Between Washington and Du Bois

UNIVERSITY PRESS OF FLORIDA

Florida A&M University, Tallahassee
Florida Atlantic University, Boca Raton
Florida Gulf Coast University, Ft. Myers
Florida International University, Miami
Florida State University, Tallahassee
New College of Florida, Sarasota
University of Central Florida, Orlando
University of Florida, Gainesville
University of North Florida, Jacksonville
University of South Florida, Tampa
University of West Florida, Pensacola

BETWEEN WASHINGTON AND DU BOIS

The Racial Politics of
James Edward Shepard

Reginald K. Ellis

UNIVERSITY PRESS OF FLORIDA

Gainesville / Tallahassee / Tampa / Boca Raton

Pensacola / Orlando / Miami / Jacksonville / Ft. Myers / Sarasota

Library of Congress Cataloging-in-Publication Data
Names: Ellis, Reginald K., author.
Title: Between Washington and Du Bois : the racial politics of James Edward
   Shepard / Reginald K. Ellis.
Description: Gainesville : University Press of Florida, 2017. | Includes
   bibliographical references and index.
Identifiers: LCCN 2017030384 | ISBN 9780813056609 (cloth : alk. paper)
Subjects: LCSH: African Americans—Social conditions—20th century. |
   Shepard, James E.—Biography. | National Religious Training School and
   Chautauqua (Durham, N.C.)—History. | African Americans—Education
   (Higher)—North Carolina. | African Americans—Southern States.
Classification: LCC E185.86 .E4364 2018 | DDC 305.896/0730904—dc23
LC record available at https://lccn.loc.gov/2017030384

The University Press of Florida is the scholarly publishing agency for the
State University System of Florida, comprising Florida A&M University,
Florida Atlantic University, Florida Gulf Coast University, Florida
International University, Florida State University, New College of Florida,
University of Central Florida, University of Florida, University of North
Florida, University of South Florida, and University of West Florida.

University Press of Florida
15 Northwest 15th Street
Gainesville, FL 32611-2079
http://upress.ufl.edu

This manuscript is dedicated to my mother, Mrs. Erma J. Mills-Ellis. Thank you for always reminding me of the importance of an education and believing in me when others refused to. (February 21, 1952–May 27, 2012)

Contents

Acknowledgments

This study on Dr. James Edward Shepard developed out of my desire to research the leadership styles of black college presidents during the Jim Crow era. As a graduate student at Florida A&M University (FAMU), I researched four college presidents: Thomas De Salle Tucker, Nathan B. Young, William H. A. Howard, and William Gray. All of these men led FAMU during the Jim Crow era. In 2006, as a graduate student at the University of Memphis, I researched Tennessee Agricultural and Industrial College's first president, William Jasper Hale and Le Moyen-Owen College's first black president, Hollis Freemen Price.

As I grew closer to completing my planning for this project, I knew that I needed to narrow the list of black college presidents so that I could focus on all aspects of the life of only one black college president during the Jim Crow era. After reading about North Carolina College's founding president in Glenda Gilmore's manuscript, *Gender and Jim Crow*, I became intrigued about James E. Shepard's leadership style in the Tar-Heel state. I decided to investigate his life, and my research on this extraordinary individual developed into this larger understanding of the role of a black college president during the early twentieth century.

During the summer of 2013, I was accepted to participate in the National Endowment for the Humanities, African American Struggles for Freedom and Civil Rights Institute held at the W.E.B. Du Bois Institute for African and African American Research at Harvard University. Over a twenty-one day period, I engaged in an intensive discourse pertaining to the idea of the "Long Civil Rights Movement" with scholars from around the nation. By the end of this journey, I gained a better understanding of the role that Shepard in specific, and black college presidents in the Deep South in general, played in the enhancement of their race during the Jim Crow era.

Throughout this journey I have incurred many debts. I am greatly appreciative of the guidance, encouragement, comments, and suggestions given to me by my mentors and friends: Dr. Beverly G. Bond, professor of history and director of African and African American Studies at the University of Memphis, provided guidance for the overall structure of the study. Dr. Charles W. Crawford, professor of history, University of Memphis, read several drafts of this manuscript and encouraged me throughout the process. I would like to give special thanks to Drs. Aram Goudsouzian, professor and chair of the Department of History at the University of Memphis, and David H. Jackson Jr., associate vice provost and dean of graduate studies at Florida A&M University, for providing timely and critical analysis of my manuscript. Both men are largely responsible for developing me into the historian I am today.

I would be remiss if I did not thank the following people: Drs. Larry E. Rivers, professor of history at Valdosta State University, Titus Brown, professor of history at Florida A&M University, and Raymond Gavins, professor of history at Duke University, for providing research and contextual advice for this work. Dr. Rivers was the first historian I personally knew. From a very early age, he mentored me both professionally and personally while constantly encouraging me to ask the tougher questions. Dr. Brown sparked the idea of researching Thomas De Salle Tucker which eventually led me to research black college presidents during the Jim Crow era. Dr. Gavins offered key analysis of my study that helped me place Shepard in a larger historical context.

Dr. Steve Ceccoli, chair of the Department of International Studies at Rhodes College, and Ms. Marva Hinton, of Mango Media, Incorporated, edited my manuscript—I am greatly indebted to Dr. Ceccoli and Ms. Hinton for their time and effort. Drs. Shirletta J. Kinchen, Jeffery Littlejohn, and Peter Levy provided analytical feedback as well encouragement throughout my research and writing process. I am also grateful to Sian Hunter of the University Press of Florida for her editorial feedback during the publishing stages of this manuscript.

In September of 2006, while serving as the Founding President of the Graduate Association of African American History (GAAAH), at the University of Memphis, I had the honor of meeting a young bright graduate student from Northwestern University. Over ten years later, Dr. Crystal R. Sanders has not only supported and encouraged me to further my research on Shepard, she has also introduced me to scholars who have provided insightful feedback on my manuscript. Such scholars as her mentor Dr. Raymond Gavins and Dr. Waldo E. Martin. Thank you, Crystal, for your years of support and friendship in seeing this manuscript come to fruition.

I would also like to acknowledge Dr. Darius J. Young, my colleague and friend of over twelve years, for his critical and analytical feedback. More importantly, thank you "Joe" for helping to keep me sane during this rigorous process. To

Dr. Maurice J. Nutt, McKinley Martin, and Edward Howard, thank you for your financial and emotional support throughout this process.

Last, none of my efforts would have been possible without the support and encouragement of my sister, LaSaundra Ellis-Peters, and my mother, Mrs. Erma J. Mills-Ellis, who served as my first research assistant. When I started this project, my mother traveled with me from Tallahassee, Florida, to Durham, North Carolina, via car to research in the archives of the Perkins Library on the campus of Duke University, the Southern Collection at the University of North Carolina at Chapel Hill, and the Special Collections at North Carolina Central University. The joy and excitement that my mother had during that week-long research trip was one that she carried with her for years, as she would tell everyone she encountered about my work on Shepard. Sadly, I did not complete this manuscript prior to my mother's transition. Nonetheless, I believe that she is as proud of this work today as she was during our first research trip over ten years ago.

Most importantly, this study would not have been possible without the support of my wife, Delexis. From the inception of this study, Delexis not only offered words of comfort and support, she also traveled with me on research trips, remained patient, and made many sacrifices over the years while still encouraging me to finishing this project. Thank you, Delexis, for keeping me focused over the past ten years. These three ladies have been my rock throughout this process, and therefore, I am grateful.

Although others provided me assistance with this study, all errors contained herein are mine alone.

Introduction

On November 3, 1875, one year and four days prior to one of the most controversial presidential elections in American history—an election that effectively ended the Reconstruction Era, the Reverend Augustus Shepard and Hattie Shepard of North Carolina welcomed the first of their twelve children into the world. Unbeknownst to James Edward Shepard, the events that were rapidly unraveling around him were to influence his life's works for decades to come.

Two years prior to his birth, the United States Supreme Court issued a ruling in the *Slaughterhouse Cases* of 1873 in which the Court decided that a citizen's privileges and immunities, protected by the Constitution's Fourteenth Amendment against the states, were limited to those written in the Constitution and did not include many rights given by the individual states. Ultimately, this case served as the catalyst for the Supreme Court's decision twenty-three years later when it decided that separate but equal accommodations were indeed constitutional in the *Plessy v. Ferguson* decision of 1896. With the federal government's influence being limited in state's affairs, southern redemption was occurring at a rapid pace. Two major Supreme Court decisions in tow, southern legislatures began to systematically restore antebellum customs to their region. Thus, the weakening of the Fourteenth Amendment helped to institutionalize state rule. For example, staunchly conservative lawmakers in the Deep South began to legally disenfranchise black southerners through the South Carolina Eight Box law of 1882, the Mississippi Plan of 1890, and Louisiana's Grandfather Clause of 1898. These tactics ensured that political power within the black community during James Shepard's era was limited at best.

This was the social and political reality into which James E. Shepard was born. For many within the black community, the perceived and realized loss of their right to vote created doubt in their ability to achieve the American Dream. Consequentially, there was a shift in attention from voting to the proper education of the black masses—with a keen focus on creating educated voters with the ability to regain the franchise for African Americans. Prior to the complete disenfranchisement of the black community, black legislators worked feverishly to establish government-supported institutions of black education. Joined with the cooperation of Southern and Colored Farmers Alliance members, public education began to take form in the South in ways that potentially benefited not only southern blacks, but poor whites as well. State support for public education was not limited to primary schools, however; the creation of higher educational institutions gained wide support during this era. While there was seemingly biracial backing for the creation of state-supported educational institutions for both white and black citizens during the last two decades of the nineteenth century, the issue of the appropriate curriculum for black students consumed this topic for a generation.

While James Shepard was still coming of age, two leading black educators were thrust into a debate that framed the early twentieth century. Historians often consider the philosophical discourse between Booker T. Washington and W. E. B. Du Bois as one of the central issues of African American history during the Progressive Era. A wave of historical scholarship has generated theories and examined high-profile proponents and critics of the ideologies of these two individuals. Washington's ideas of higher education for the black race were crafted from General Samuel Chapman Armstrong's curriculum at the Hampton Institute. This curriculum focused primarily on vocational and industrial training. Privilege and opportunity were the chief reasons for Du Bois' arguments in favor of classical education. This concept centered on Bishop Henry L. Morehouse's idea of the talented tenth. Morehouse argued for the education of at least 10 percent of the African American population who would then train the masses in Protestant values with the ultimate outcome aimed at subduing the desire for an African American revolt against white Americans. Du Bois tailored Morehouse's concept of the talented tenth to best suit the needs of the race by arguing that an advantaged 10 percent of the African American community should receive liberal arts training and return to their society as community leaders and educators. Here lies the division in the scholarly arena as to which concept was best suited for the advancement of the race, Washington's vocational and industrial model or Du Bois' talented-tenth concept.[1]

Washington's argument for vocational and industrial education targeted the majority of the African American population, a populace that was only thirty years removed from the shackles of slavery. His goal for this form of education was to create the spirit of self-help among the masses. James D. Anderson's *The Education of Blacks in the South* (1988) argues that Washington and those who followed his teachings integrated industrial training into their curriculum so that their pupils would understand the importance of hard work. Washington's approach trained his students to become self-sufficient in the production of the essentials for their overall survival without becoming overly reliant on southern white Americans for foodstuffs and other basic needs. Many of the early, publicly funded black colleges and universities were either industrial or agricultural and mechanical institutions. Anderson contends that colleges of this sort only provided rudimentary instruction because of the perceived notion that their students were not developing critical thinking skills—that they were, rather, honing skills in industry and agriculture. These institutions of supposedly higher education provided survival techniques. These were the institutions that most local and national political officials supported for black higher education, since they appeared to "train better Negroes, not smarter ones."[2]

While technical training for African Americans was generally accepted by the white community and conservative black leaders of the late nineteenth and early twentieth centuries, black colleges that focused on liberal arts education, such as black privately funded institutions like Fisk University in Nashville, Tennessee, and Morehouse College in Atlanta, Georgia, liberal arts instruction was the rule of the day. These colleges were considered the trainers of critical thinkers, thus advancing the race at a more rapid pace. These were the institutions that followed Du Bois's model of educating a talented tenth of the black population that would then serve as leaders for the entire race.[3]

Recent scholarship attempts to place the presidents of black liberal arts colleges at the center of the Washington–Du Bois debate by arguing that a number of these educators openly refuted Washington's ideology. Leroy Davis's biography of John Hope, president of Morehouse College, argues that Hope was the "Booker T. Washington of liberal arts education," which in Davis's view made Hope as influential in educating black students in liberal arts education as Washington was to industrial education. It is difficult to disagree that Hope played an influential role in the development of young African American minds in this country, or even that he reached the iconic level as described by John Hope Franklin in his autobiography, *A Mirror to America* (2005). However, Hope and his philosophy of black higher education never reached the magnitude of support that Washington gained for his industrial education philosophy. Washington garnered administrative positions and financial support for black college presidents throughout the South. Washington supported, for instance, William Jasper Hale of Tennessee Agricultural and Normal State College, in Nashville, Tennessee; Nathan Benjamin Young of the Florida Agricultural & Mechanical College for Negroes, in Tallahassee, Florida; and James Edward Shepard at the

North Carolina College for Negroes in Durham, North Carolina. These men and others were either approved by or received acceptance from Washington as state officials inquired about their worth in pushing the issue of proper education for African Americans. Many of these leaders walked a fine line between the philosophies of Washington and Du Bois. When necessary, they were advocates of industrial education as well as liberal arts instruction. These administrators subscribed to whatever program advanced their school at that time. When historians attempt to place more emphasis on which ideology was the most pertinent for African Americans, they overlook the central theme of both theories, which was to advance the race in the early twentieth century.[4]

The life of James Shepard provides a unique interpretation of the role of a black college president during the Jim Crow Era. Specifically, Shepard, during his early thirties established a private liberal arts educational institution, which eventually was absorbed by the state of North Carolina nearly fifteen years later. This made the North Carolina College for Negroes the first state-supported black college with a liberal arts curriculum in the South. Scholars of the Jim Crow Era have grappled with the concept of how Shepard was able to maintain a liberal arts agenda in the Jim Crow South during this era, while also benefiting from the support of both Washington and Du Bois.

This question is best answered by providing insight into Shepard's upbringing. The privilege of being born into a leading southern black family offered the young man many advantages. For example, as a youth Shepard was able to enroll in the model department, equivalent to a preparatory school, of Shaw University in Raleigh, North Carolina, at the age of eight due to his father's status as a prominent minister in North Carolina. Shortly thereafter he completed his primary training under the tutelage of his uncle at the Shiloh Institute in Warrenton, North Carolina; then he enrolled in the pharmaceutical department of Shaw University, where he graduated in 1894 at the age of nineteen. Equipped with his degree, James became one of the first African American druggists in North Carolina, a profession in which he excelled for three years before he changed career paths.[5]

In 1897 he was appointed as the chief clerk in the Recorder of Deeds office in Washington, DC. A year later he became deputy collector of internal revenue in Raleigh, North Carolina. In this position, Shepard was able to strengthen his connections with influential whites in Durham and throughout North Carolina, ties that were previously established through his father's role as a leading minister in the state. After several years of governmental service, Shepard's religious calling led him to accept the position as the field superintendent for the International Sunday School Association. This was his first opportunity at advancing blacks through education. His job was to "improve Sunday Schools in management, methods, and equipments; and to endeavor to bring the denominations into a closer understanding for cooperation to uplift the race." In this position, Shepard saw the need for properly educating African American ministers, many of whom he found ill equipped for their positions and largely illiterate at the turn of the twentieth century. With the help of Durham's black and white communities, he opened the National Religious Training Institute and Chautauqua (NRTIC) in 1910, predecessor of North Carolina Central University, to elevate blacks both morally and educationally.[6]

The concept of enhancing the morality of the black community via education was not unique to Shepard. Leaders of the black upper class during the age of accommodation presumed the best way to defeat white supremacy was to prove that African Americans were socially, politically, and educationally equal to their white counterparts. Therefore, these leaders desired not only to drive illiteracy out of the black community, but also to exile common vices that were deemed immoral—such as vagrancy, failure to attend church, and being unemployed.[7]

Black leaders preferred to be in the forefront of advancing their race by tackling the aforementioned depravities during a time when world-renowned poet Rudyard Kipling published his famous poem "The White Man's Burden: The United States and the Philippine Islands," in the *New York Sun* on February 10, 1899. Kipling's elegy was not well received for its poetic acumen, but its words caused white American political and business officials to heed its charge. Specifically, politicians such as the US senator from South Carolina, Ben Tillman, and the future president of the United States, Theodore Roosevelt, to regard Kipling's poem as an exhortation not only in support of America's imperialist aims, but also white Americans' desire to civilize nonwhites in America. Black leaders at the turn of the twentieth century argued that they were best suited to "ease the white man's burden" by taking the lead in advancing their race. By doing this, these leaders assumed that under their guidance, the black community would prove itself civilized and equal to white Americans.[8]

Therefore, at the close of the nineteenth century, a number of prominent African American leaders throughout the country, especially in the South, focused on an ideology that they termed *racial uplift*. While this term on the surface appears beneficial to the masses of the black community, the ultimate desire of these black leaders was to remove the negative imagery of African Americans as the standard for their race. However, many racial uplifters themselves used racist stereotypes to promote their particular avenues for advancing the race.[9]

For example, Booker T. Washington, the educator from the rural town of Tuskegee, Alabama, appealed to northern white Christian philanthropists to fund his institution in 1890 by arguing that the masses of southern black ministers were ill equipped to preach the word of God to their parishioners. Therefore, he argued that his institution would incorporate the civilizing mission into its overall agenda, which would ultimately ease the white man's burden. This idea of a civilizing mission played on the beliefs of many white Christians who assumed that African Americans were devoid of true religion and moral character. Therefore, it was the desire of the racial uplifters to endow the masses of the black community with morality through various avenues. Such paths included the creation of community centers and black women's clubs like the Atlanta Neighborhood Union, Young Women's Christian Association (YWCA), and the National Association of Colored Women (NACW). These groups focused on creating the Victorian Lady model in the black community at the turn of the twentieth century. Also, during this time several institutions of higher education for African Americans were founded for the purpose of training people of color to be efficient, independent workers in the twentieth century, while also being analytical thinkers.[10]

Washington was not the only African American to use negative depictions of the black community to garner support for his approach toward racial uplift. An array of the early black elites used similar strategies to define how different they were from the masses of the black community. Collectively, their ultimate desire was to uplift the race by enumerating the negative portrayals of the race. After doing that, the members of the black elite explained the similarities that they had with the white middle-class: obtaining an education, being a Christian, and having a job. This ultimately led to their overall argument for advancing the race that was based on the fundamental premise that they (the black elite) could raise the standards of the masses by helping the latter assimilate to the elite's existing class level. While some scholars view this ideology from a theoretical approach by revealing the complicated layers of racial uplift, this book views the uplift ideology through the lens of James E. Shepard, the founding president of present-day North Carolina Central University, to divulge the complexities that led him to his views of racial uplift and morality.[11]

Often in the discourse of racial uplift, scholars focus on business, community, and religious leaders. Numerous biographies and autobiographies have been written revealing how influential African Americans attempted to elevate the race by using their positions in society. Other works about advancing African Americans deal with the most effective manner of elevating the race, while wrestling with the idea of what Du Bois considered the double consciousness of the black community during the twentieth century, a consciousness that he described as a "two-ness, an American, a Negro; two warring ideals in one dark body, whose dogged strength alone keeps it from being torn asunder." This double consciousness led prominent African Americans to the brink of emotional meltdown, as they continuously found themselves not being welcomed in the mainstream American community, yet being disconnected from the black community for having a higher social, educational, and economic status. Nonetheless, this scholarship still finds its way back to the famous Washington–Du Bois dispute, as historians have elevated this discourse from debates over educational philosophies to arguments about which segment of the black community could properly lead the race from the darkness of racial prejudice and segregation into the light of self-sufficiency and universal belonging.[12]

This monograph chronicles the life of James E. Shepard from 1875 until his death in 1947 by analyzing his approach to racial uplift during the Jim Crow Era. Scholars of the early Jim Crow Era have broadly labeled the time frame from 1895 until 1915 the age of Booker T. Washington. Specifically, researchers claimed that black leaders in this era were conservative race leaders at best, accommodationist at worst. Due to the influence of Washington, the Wizard of Tuskegee, historians have attempted to frame the works of the southern black professional class by comparing them to his actions. With more analysis current scholarship is beginning to trend away from that paradigm. For example, Blair L. M. Kelley encourages researchers to reexamine late nineteenth- and early twentieth-century movements and leaders in the context of their time rather than comparing them to leaders and movements that transpired decades later. In doing this, one will find it difficult to label leaders of this era as conservative or accommodationist.[13]

James E. Shepard of North Carolina, like Booker T. Washington in Alabama, was one of the most influential African Americans in his state during his life. Shepard's desire to advance the race dates back to his years as a pharmacist, tax collector, and co-founder of the North Carolina Mutual Life Insurance Company. His early approach to the race issue was more aggressive than in later years. After becoming president of the NRTIC, his responsibilities in Durham's black community grew. Unlike Washington, however, Shepard lived during a time when although conservative race leaders were common, a militant race leader gained acceptance in the public eye. Scholars often wonder if Washington's approach to the race issue would have lasted had he lived longer. No such questions about Shepard have arisen as he began his career as a college president in 1910 and remained one until his death in 1947. This work argues that his position on the issue of race issue never wavered. However, his approach to solving the problem of Jim Crow evolved as he gained more responsibility for his institution.[14]

For example, one year prior to the opening of the NRTIC, Oswald Garrison Villard, the grandson of William Lloyd Garrison, along with fellow white progressives Mary White Ovington and William English Walling issued the call for the creation of the National Association for the Advancement of Colored People. This beckoning occurred due to the horrific race riot that took place in Springfield, Illinois, in 1908. A number of leading black citizens began to demand antilynching legislation, a demand never delivered on. Nonetheless, from the beginning of this organization, well into the late 1920s, Shepard was a proud supporter of the NAACP and its civil rights agenda. His efforts in support of the association were lauded in the mid-1920s as he was nominated for the Spingarn Award by the NAACP's membership.

As leadership of this civil rights organization changed, so did the group's agenda. As early as the late 1920s, under the leadership of Walter White, the NAACP not only shifted its support from the Republican Party to the Democratic Party but also began to push for social equality in higher education. This new agenda placed Shepard and other publically funded black colleges on a collision course with the nation's preeminent civil rights organization.

Glenda Gilmore, Robert Cannon, Christina Greene, and Sarah Thuesen, have all cited displeasure that the black community felt toward Shepard and the way he handled racial equality issues while serving as president of the North Carolina College for Negroes (NCC). He blocked Thomas Hocutt, a graduate of NCC, from integrating the University of North Carolina's pharmacy program by simply withholding his transcript. Strategies of this sort allowed Shepard to receive funds for professional programs at NCC, which he believed would ultimately develop the race further than integration by providing greater professional opportunities for black North Carolinians. The NAACP, and in particular Walter White, dismissed Shepard as an ally in the 1930s in the fight to integrate higher education in North Carolina. These attacks did not alter Shepard's vision of uplift as the racial atmosphere evolved during his administration.[15]

This manuscript will also add to the body of scholarship on black college presidents. Previous works have dealt with this subject by examining the day-to-day activities of these individuals with major emphasis placed on their role as administrators at their institutions. These works have also focused on the colleges they led rather than the individual leaders themselves. One of the best works on a black college president is Gerald L. Smith's biography of Kentucky State College president Rufus B. Atwood. Smith argues that Atwood "walked the tightrope" to gain both financial and political support from both the white and black communities for his institution. A biography of an early black college president that steps outside of this administrative model is Leroy Davis's *A Clashing of the Soul* (1998). This work reveals how John Hope grappled with his personal racial identity while serving as a race leader. Although not mixed race like Hope, Shepard also wrestled with the proper way to advance the race at a time when militancy became the rule of the day.[16]

The purpose of this manuscript is threefold. First, it will serve as a cultural biography of Dr. James Edward Shepard and the National Religious Training Institute and Chautauqua for the Negro Race and later the North Carolina College for Negroes. Second, it will argue that black college presidents of the early twentieth century such as Shepard were more than academic leaders; they were also race leaders. Shepard's role at the NRTIC/NCC was to develop a race through this institution. Lastly, this study argues that Shepard, like most black college presidents, did not focus primarily on the difference between liberal arts and vocational education. Rather, he considered the most practical ways to uplift his race. Therefore, this study will be more than a biography of an influential African American, but rather an analytical study of a black leader during the age of Jim Crow in the South.

1

The Emergence of a Black Leader during the Age of Jim Crow and Black Racial Uplift in North Carolina

James Edward Shepard was born on November 3, 1875. A year after his birth, the United States was bracing itself for another internal conflict eleven years after the Civil War's end. This time a historic presidential election served as the boiling point as white southerners were primed to regain what they considered their rightful place in society. At the same time, African Americans' new role in the political and business arenas led to their desire to elect an individual who would ultimately expand the gains that were made during Reconstruction. With the rise in unprosecuted race-based hate crimes in the South and a spike in terrorist activities such as those initiated by the Ku Klux Klan, many black leaders demanded a president who would continue to protect their human and civil rights. However, neither of the two major presidential candidates, former Ohio governor Republican Rutherford B. Hayes and former New York governor Democrat Samuel J. Tilden, were interested in the African American vote. During this election, the Red Shirt Democrats proclaimed that they would help to redeem the South, while the "Party of Lincoln" turned its back on its former black constituency, ultimately focusing its attention on a more white, conservative base. As the Republican Party began to use tactics of white solidarity similar to those of the Democratic Party to gain votes, the presidential election of 1876 became more heated. Eventually, it took a compromise (Hayes and the Republicans allowed southern states to regain home rule) for Hayes to be elected president over Tilden. This compromise restored southern states' rights and removed federal troops from the South, which soon ended the remnants of Reconstruction in that region.[1]

This was the racial and political era in which James Edward Shepard was born into in 1875 and which shaped his future role in society. James Shepard's environment influenced his work and his perspective on racial uplift at an early age. This atmosphere led Shepard to grapple with the most effective way of advancing the race at the dawn of the twentieth century. In short, he contemplated whether black advancement could be achieved through demands for equal rights or through the gradual tactics that were employed by black leaders during this era.

If the compromise of 1877 serves as the backdrop of James Shepard's life, the institution of slavery provides context for the lives of his parents, Augustus Shepard and Hattie Whitted Shepard. Augustus Shepard was born in Raleigh, North Carolina, in 1846 to Richard and Flora Shepard, who were both slaves in the state's capital city. Growing up enslaved in the antebellum South filled Augustus with rage, an energy he later suppressed with a higher calling. Twenty years after his birth and one year after slavery was abolished, a religious revival occurred in Raleigh where Augustus "proclaimed faith in God." In April 1866, the Reverend William Warrick, the first black Baptist preacher of that city, baptized Shepard. Augustus's early zeal for spiritual righteousness would later play a large role in the lives of all of his children, especially that of his son, James, who eventually created an educational institution for the training of black preachers.[2]

Augustus heeded this higher calling, enrolling in Raleigh's Baptist Institute (the present-day Shaw University) in 1869. It was at this institution that Augustus gained his theological training under the tutelage of Reverend Henry M. Tupper, president of the school. Tupper, a white minister from Massachusetts, was a graduate of the Newton Theological Seminary and was affiliated with the American Baptist Home Missionary Society (ABHMS). After graduating from the seminary in 1862, Tupper wanted to serve the religious needs of African Americans. Consequently, at the close of the Civil War he traveled south to do missionary work with the former slaves in Raleigh under the auspices of the ABHMS. He later opened a theological school in that city for blacks. The strategies that President Tupper used to finance the school were similar to those later employed by James Shepard when he founded a religious institution in Durham a generation later. Augustus once was appointed by the student body to conduct a special service of prayer for a financial donation for the school. Any time the school found itself in financial straits, the president would write for funds and ask the students for their prayers. One story that Augustus must have passed along to his family was Tupper's ability to secure pledges from northern businessmen, who sent large financial gifts to the institution. For example, in 1870 Tupper received a $5,000 donation from Elijah Shaw, a woolen manufacturer from Wales, Massachusetts, for the purchase of land, which helped to expand Tupper's school. Due to this generous "gift and later ones," the school was named in honor of Shaw.[3]

Under Tupper's tutelage, Augustus became more connected with his spirituality. After graduating from the institute, he accepted the pastorate of one of the black Baptist churches in Hillsboro, North Carolina. While in this position, Augustus gained respect from both the white and black communities as a man of sterling worth because of the services that he rendered to his congregation. During his rise to local prominence, African Americans from rural areas of North Carolina migrated into urban areas of the state and throughout the country. For example, during the 1870s, the proportion of blacks in Raleigh rose from 44 percent to 50 percent. Moreover, an undercount of African Americans in urban areas during that decade's census likely made the latter actual percentage even greater. As rural "uneducated" blacks moved to the city, educated black ministers were expected to provide a source of inspirational and spiritual guidance and also serve as "intermediaries between the black and white worlds of the city." That was when Augustus's star rose. He not only provided theological guidance for his flock but also gave opportunities for his congregation within the city that they would not have had if not for the respect he earned from the white community during the post-Reconstruction years. This respectability paid off for James Shepard in later years. White philanthropists like Benjamin Newton Duke occasionally referenced their esteem for Augustus Shepard when dealing with his son, James.[4]

At an ecclesiastical gathering in the 1870s, Augustus met a devout young woman by the name of Hattie E. Whitted, who was born in Hillsboro, North Carolina, on April 12, 1858. Overwhelmed by her beauty and devotion to her faith, Rev. Shepard began courting young Hattie, a courtship that led the couple to marriage in 1875 in Greensboro, North Carolina. Early in this young relationship, individuals around the Shepards saw the love they shared for each other and the dedication they had in "spreading the Word of God." According to Augustus's biographer J. A. Whitted, the brother of Hattie, "everyone who entered [the Shepard home] was deeply impressed at the scriptural rule, and that was the rule and guide of [their] home."[5] These standards were solidly in place by the time these honeymooners had their first of twelve children, James Edward Shepard.

The Shepards inculcated James with a heavy dose of spiritual and religious training and emphasized the importance of obtaining a proper education. Young James was enrolled in the model department, a preparatory school, of Shaw University in Raleigh at the age of eight. After years of early educational training in the model department at Shaw, the younger Shepard began studying under the tutelage of his uncle at the Shiloh Institute in Warrenton, North Carolina.

After completing his primary education, James enrolled in the pharmaceutical department of Shaw University, graduating in 1894 at the age of nineteen. In doing so, he became one of the first African American druggists in the state of North Carolina. He excelled in this profession for three years before eventually changing career paths.[6]

One year after completing his degree, James Shepard met a young lady who would later become his close associate in his life's work. Annie Day Robinson was no ordinary woman, and young Shepard could not simply use his intellect or clout as a black pharmacist to impress her. Annie's grandfather was Thomas Day, an African American furniture tycoon from North Carolina. After a courtship that likely included the approval of both Annie's and James's parents, the couple made their relationship official by getting married on November 7, 1895, four days after James celebrated his twentieth birthday. Neither Shepard nor Robinson was marrying up or down on the social ladder. Their nuptials were more of a horizontal nature as the Shepards were a respected family within both the black and white communities in central North Carolina, while the Day family garnered the same respect from North Carolinians of both races due to the esteem that Thomas Day earned as an artisan. A marriage of this sort was the rule of the day for the black elite or for individuals who aspired to be a part of that group. To guarantee their family's status in the black elite, it was customary for these individuals to marry into families that had strong social and financial status during the late nineteenth century.[7]

Newly married and armed with a pharmacy degree, Shepard was in high demand both personally and professionally. He worked in Charlotte and Durham, North Carolina, as well as in Danville, Virginia. In contrast to North Carolina, where African Americans were not completely disenfranchised until 1900, Virginia had laid the foundation for African American disenfranchisement nine years before Shepard even earned his pharmacy degree. An event that took place in Danville in 1883 highlighted the racial etiquette required in that state. As African Americans began to step out of their place during Reconstruction by openly revealing and implementing their desire for the vote, racial tension escalated. Such tension eventually led to a massacre when a "white mob shot into a crowd of unarmed black men, women and children." Sadly, as racial roles continued to change in Virginia, white traditionalists wanted to redeem their positions of supremacy in that city that had been lost during the Reconstruction Era. After the riot, "white Democrats then took control of the city and spread rumors of black insurrection throughout the state."[8] This event, according to historian Jane Dailey, muffled any hope the African American community had of gaining political capital in Virginia during the election of 1883. Furthermore, after this successful display of intimidation in Virginia, the use of violence in politics spread from state to state in a manner that discouraged African Americans from participating in the political process altogether.

In the 1890s, a combination of events likely influenced Shepard's decision to step away from the pharmacy profession. In 1895, one year before he left his pharmacy position, Booker T. Washington delivered his famous address at the Atlanta Cotton States Exposition. Washington encouraged the black southerners, only thirty years removed from the shackles of slavery, to "cast down [their] buckets" by working in vocations or moral labor, an idea that tied into his approach to racial uplift. The emerging race leader used his double-talk ability to inform his audience of black and white listeners that both races desired a form of de facto segregation. He proclaimed that "in all things that are purely social we can be as separate as the fingers, yet one as the hand in all things essential to mutual progress." It was also during this speech that higher education for African Americans was clearly defined for white Americans by this prominent black leader. The roles of publicly funded black colleges in the South were soon changed to fit into Washington's model of vocational and industrial education. At the dawn of the Industrial Revolution in the United States, the larger community perceived these schools as training a "better Negro, not a smarter one." Yet because Washington placed education before civil rights, some prominent black leaders throughout the country attacked him for accommodating the white power structure.[9]

During the later years of his presidency at the North Carolina College for Negroes, James Shepard endured similar criticism. Much of this condemnation was caused by some of the accommodating positions that Shepard took as it pertained to his institution. One such position manifested itself when he withheld Thomas Hocutt's transcript, which ultimately denied Hocutt's admittance into the University of North Carolina pharmacy school. Another source of complaint for Shepard's critics centered on his relationships with white benefactors in both the public and private sectors. Like Washington, Shepard courted white public officials during the founding and maintenance of the National Religious Training Institute and Chautauqua for the Negro Race (NRTIC). Also like Washington, Shepard received major financial support for his institution from prominent white businessmen. While Shepard and Washington gained the support of white philanthropists, they also paid a political cost, since some radicals in their own communities viewed them as accommodationists. Despite this negative backlash, each received funds that ensured the longevity of their schools. While Washington and Shepard had their share of critics for some decisions they made (or did not make), they also had a strong contingent of loyalists such as the Bookerites and the array of black Durhamites who viewed Shepard as a "god" in their communities. These individuals believed that Shepard and Washington were advancing the race through the tactics they were employing.[10]

Shepard wrestled with the state of racial affairs in North Carolina during the 1890s. African Americans in that state braced themselves for their total disenfranchisement. Fusionists—Republicans and Populists—controlled the political arena in North Carolina, while white redeemers desired to cleanse the Tar Heel State of liberal white and black politicians altogether. Urged on by radical Democrats, conservative newspapers such as Durham's *Tobacco Plant* incited a propaganda campaign that provoked fears on the part of white moderates against their Fusionist enemy. This pro-Confederate barrage continued well into the late 1890s, culminating in 1898 with the Wilmington Race Riot.[11]

In an attempt to rid Wilmington of African American politicians and businessmen, white redeemers furiously roamed that city in search of the aforementioned black leaders. In an expression of his support for such actions, Alfred Moore Wadell, a former Confederate and current United States representative, "vowed in a speech to choke the Cape Fear River with carcasses." After this violent storm settled, at least twelve black men had been murdered. Shortly thereafter, more than 1,500 African American residents of Wilmington deserted that city, leaving behind valuable property and a once-peaceful life. Without objection, some of the same white radicals who instigated and participated in this riot purchased the homes and property of the African Americans who fled the city for safety, ensuring that they would not soon return.[12]

During this time, African Americans were also battling the new social construction of Negrophobia. This concept, according to C. Vann Woodward and John Hope Franklin, was based on the argument that African American men in power would ultimately rape white women. With this phobia in place, the new issue of the twentieth century became more solidly the problem of the color line, as W. E. B. Du Bois would later proclaim. Sentiments of this sort led Shepard to argue more angrily for the rights of black men as early as 1900 by stating, "We recognize the fact there can be no middle ground between freedom and slavery." Finishing this fiery statement, the young man concluded by asserting, "We cannot see that the best way to make a good man is to unman him." This outcry from Shepard stemmed from the total disenfranchisement of the black male in North Carolina by 1900.[13]

Shepard made this argument not only because African American men were losing their franchise, but also because black women were uniting with white women in attempts to gain women's suffrage, which was achieved nineteen years later. He believed that with black men being legally disenfranchised while black women joined white women to gain the vote for women, leadership in the black community would shift from men to women, further unmanning black men. Therefore, as a prominent black man during the Victorian Age, Shepard obviously agreed with the sentiments of other prominent black men of the day (such as John Hope of Atlanta) that black men should be at the forefront of the cause of advancing the race. Moreover, Shepard argued that this "unmanning" of the black male would not only weaken the African American man but would weaken the black community in general by not having a true male presence advocating the advancement of the race.[14]

With the disenfranchisement of the black male in North Carolina sparking more fervor from Shepard, young businessmen and other prominent black leaders in the state devised a plan to move the race forward in the next century. These black leaders used Booker T. Washington's argument of self-help as their philosophy of advancing the race. On October 20, 1898, three years after Washington delivered his most widely circulated speech, the North Carolina Mutual and Provident Association (NCMPA)—predecessor of the North Carolina Mutual Life Insurance Company—was organized. The company began operations on April 1, 1899. The creation of the NCMPA was another early attempt by Shepard and the other prominent black leaders in North Carolina to usher black North Carolinians into the twentieth century by capitalizing on one of Washington's theories of advancing the race.[15]

Along with Pinckey William Dawkins, Edward Austin Johnson, John Merrick, Aaron Moore, William Gaston Pearson, and Dock Watson, Shepard created a black life insurance company. The early goal of this enterprise was more than self-enrichment for investors. It was to provide affordable life insurance to individuals who previously had not been covered and "to provide employment opportunities [that were] not available elsewhere." Moreover, the early motto of the company was "Merciful to All," which directly tied into the company's objectives of providing "relief [to] the widows and orphans," with funds given to the Colored Orphan Asylum at Oxford, North Carolina. Shepard and his partners not only focused on enhancing their own financial status but also on the social and financial well-being of the black citizens of their city.[16]

During the late nineteenth century, most African Americans who actually had life insurance received it through their membership in fraternal organizations such as the Prince Hall Free and Accepted Masons (PH F&AM) or the Order of Eastern Stars (OES). A number of the founders of the NCMPA were prominent Masons. Shepard in later years was the Grand Master Mason of North Carolina. Prior to Shepard's rise in Masonry, two of the co-founders of the NCMPA, John Merrick and William Pearson, were officers of their fraternal benefit society. Merrick was Supreme Grand Master of the Royal Knights of King David and Pearson, the Supreme Grand Secretary of the society. According to North Carolina Mutual's historian, William Kennedy, the Royal Knights had established "lodges even in the State of Virginia, where two Negro industrial life insurance companies had already been formed." This point not only underscores the importance that Shepard and the co-founders of NCMPA placed on life insurance for African Americans but also on the role that fraternal societies such as the Prince Hall F&AM played in the black community during the late nineteenth and early twentieth centuries. These organizations were more than societies for social gatherings; they were institutions used to advance the race.[17]

According to historian Anna S. Butler, the existence of black "private" benevolent societies caused anxiety within the white community as there was no way of truly understanding these gatherings. For example, "secret signs[,] rituals[, and] special uniforms with symbols and regalia" frightened the white community, which had no way of decoding these "clandestine" signals. During Reconstruction, white Americans encouraged the building of churches and schools for African Americans as not only a place for community gatherings that would provide racial harmony and instruction but also as venues where African Americans could be easily watched. Nevertheless, the underlying goal of many benevolent societies during the mid- and late nineteenth century was to provide appropriate burial sites and money for funeral expenses for their communities. Butler argues that the desire of African Americans to properly bury their families "stems from the belief that the soul of a black would eventually return to the mother continent" only if the body was given a proper and respectful funeral. Therefore, prior to the creation of black life insurance companies such as the NCMPA, African Americans turned to fraternal societies to give themselves and their families a proper send-off in hopes that their souls would return home.[18]

Although the overall purpose of the NCMPA was to promote racial self-help and to provide proper burial for African Americans in Durham, the investors still wanted to create financial capital through such an organization. Unfortunately, by 1900 "the Association experienced considerable difficulty in meeting its obligations, as the ratio of sick claims to premium income" was greater than it had been during the first six months of its operations. Therefore, the original founders (with the exception of John Merrick and Aaron Moore) terminated their connection with the firm. This course of action left James Shepard in limbo. In effect, Shepard was now confronted with an important career decision. On the one hand, he grappled with his role as an investor in the NCMPA. On the other, he wrestled with the proper way to support the African American community while also supporting his young family. At the dawn of the twentieth century, Shepard once again found himself searching for his true calling.[19]

Prior to the restructuring of the NCMPA, Shepard accepted a government position as the deputy collector of the US Internal Revenue Service in Raleigh, a post that he likely earned due to his status in the Republican Party of North Carolina. Shepard and other founders of the NCMPA began to make other business plans for their future. With the survival of the association in doubt, Shepard possibly existed in a state of uncertainty, since he had left his pharmacy practice to accept the governmental position and focus on the creation of the NCMPA. Desiring to ensure a solid foundation for his family, Shepard turned back to his pharmacy roots in 1899 with the hope of opening a drugstore in Durham two years after his wife gave birth to their first child, Marjorie Augusta Shepard. Lacking the personal finances and recognizing the reorganization of the NCMPA, Shepard turned to white philanthropists to fund his pharmacy business venture. This was one of the first opportunities that the young leader had to employ the strategies of previous members of black elites such as his father. Also, this new business venture of Shepard's promoted the idea of racial self-help in the black community. The drugstore reflected the NCMPA's purpose of not only helping to bolster Shepard's personal wealth but also providing employment opportunities for black citizens of Durham. Moreover, an African American–owned and –operated pharmacy in Durham brought a sense of racial pride to a black community struggling with the new social norms of the Jim Crow Era. Using his position as the deputy collector for the US Internal Revenue Service, Shepard wrote key figures in the state hoping that they would help fund his pharmacy.[20]

Having made contact with key politicians and businessmen in North Carolina through his new government position, Shepard mailed off his first request for funds to James Stagg of Durham. Stagg's father, Francis Asbury Stagg, was the secretary-treasurer of the North Carolina Railroad Company and was the nephew of Washington Duke, the founder of the Duke Tobacco Corporation in North Carolina. His mother, Sarah Durham Stagg, was the sister of Bartlett

Durham, the man for whom the city of Durham was named. The Duke family eventually became major contributors to Shepard's school during the early twentieth century, likely due to the bonds that Shepard and Stagg had forged during the late nineteenth and early twentieth centuries.[21]

In his first letter to James Stagg, which was written on Internal Revenue Service letterhead, Shepard informed Stagg that he was "quite anxious to go into the drug business again." In an attempt to inform this potential lender of his need for funds, Shepard told Stagg that he could purchase the "Durham Drug Company for $2,100," of which the former owner required $1,850 in cash. Shepard asked for $5,100, which he thought he could pay back with interest within three years. To entice his prospective lender, Shepard informed Stagg that he would "give a mortgage in $800 worth of personal property and a second mortgage in real estate for $500." Thinking that these amounts might not be sufficient, Shepard appeared willing to use his life insurance policy as collateral in his appeal to Stagg. He informed the philanthropist that he would "give a $2,000, [twenty] payment life insurance [policy], which I have been carrying for three years." This was likely a policy that Shepard had with the now-struggling NCMPA. In the end, however, Stagg refused to fund Shepard's venture. It is not clear if Stagg was familiar with the financial status of the insurance company, but it may have played a large role in his decision not to fund Shepard's request.[22]

It has not been clearly ascertained why James Stagg denied Shepard's appeal for funds to open a drugstore, but it does appear that through the spring of 1899 their relationship was somewhat strained. On June 7, 1899, Shepard wrote to Stagg requesting a meeting to discuss monetary matters. In this note, Shepard informed Stagg that he had been traveling on "Revenue business"; therefore, he was unable to respond quickly to previous letters sent by Stagg. In an attempt to reconcile with Stagg, Shepard encouraged a face-to-face meeting, stating that "if you will allow me the time I asked for in my previous letter, I will be able to come . . . and will endeavor to give you no further trouble." Shepard clearly believed that this situation called for a more personal touch rather than the back-and-forth communications that had caused this business relationship to become fragile. He also understood that if he ruined his relationship with James Stagg, who was not only a member of the Duke family but also the confidential secretary and agent for the Duke Tobacco Company, there would be no future relationship with the Dukes at all. Therefore, Shepard's plea for a personal meeting appeared to have been more reconciliatory than anything.[23]

With his relationship with James Stagg somewhat strained due to the lack of prompt repayment of loans, Shepard, now employed by President Theodore Roosevelt's administration in the Internal Revenue Service, began to shift his career focus from the business sector to the spiritual arena. First, however, Shepard's friend, Aaron Moore, called on him to write a letter requesting funds from Benjamin Newton Duke on Moore's behalf. In doing so, Shepard was able to maintain a relationship with the Duke family. On August 13, 1902, Shepard wrote Duke on behalf of Moore requesting a loan of $1,000 that would be paid off in three years. Shepard also informed Duke that a local banker had already turned down the two because they wanted to repay the loan sooner than three years. While this note began on the behalf of Moore, it ended with a personal appeal from Shepard for funds totaling $3,600, which Shepard argued would "put me on my feet, clean me of my debt, and start me in business." This was Shepard's last attempt to secure funds for his business venture in Durham, which was denied. Although Shepard did not succeed in obtaining funds for this business venture, Stagg approved other, smaller loans. For example, in October 1904 Shepard responded to a note from Stagg informing Duke's confidential secretary that he would "pay a part of [his] indebtedness to Mr. Duke on the 1st of November and some every month hereafter until paid." These financial loans show the early confidence the Duke family had in Shepard personally while simultaneously appearing uneasy about his ability to operate a business.[24]

Benjamin Duke's confidence in Shepard was tested again as he received yet another appeal from the young man. In this correspondence, however, Shepard requested a recommendation, not finances. This note of reference was for the position of field secretary of the International Sunday School Association (ISSA). Shepard informed Duke that "the Sunday School has decided to offer two colored men as field secretaries to labor among the colored people of the South." Shepard went on to reveal that he had already been endorsed by leading citizens of Durham and believed that a line from Duke would ensure this position for him. His request may have appeared outlandish to some during this era, but for Shepard a note from the Duke family would provide the perfect touch. From Shepard's standpoint, the strength in B. N. Duke's letter was not based on the funds that he had donated to charitable organizations but rather on the role that the Dukes played in the spiritual community of North Carolina.[25]

Washington Duke, the patriarch of the Duke family, was a devout Methodist, and his entire family joined the Methodist church shortly after their arrival in Durham in 1874. After years of dedicated membership to Trinity Methodist Church, Washington Duke and his family moved their membership to the Main Street Methodist Episcopal Church where they had donated land on which the building was constructed in 1886. Shortly after moving into their new church home, Washington Duke served as the supervisor of the Sunday schools. His son, B. N. Duke, served as the secretary-treasurer for Main Street Methodist. With one of the Methodist Church's doctrines during the Gilded Age calling for its wealthy parishioners to manage their funds wisely while also helping the downtrodden, the relationship between the Duke family and James Shepard had only just begun.[26]

It has yet to be ascertained whether James Shepard secured a letter of recommendation from Benjamin N. Duke, but what is known is that by 1900, Shepard began his service as the field secretary of ISSA. In this role, Shepard represented the state of North Carolina at the association's annual meetings, which allowed him the opportunity to travel to countries as far away as Italy, experiencing the role that religion played in various communities. Moreover, it was in this organization that the young man strengthened his relationship with a future ally and fellow black Republican, Colonel James H. Young, who was also an official of ISSA. Young had reached his prominence by delivering the black vote of North Carolina to Republican governor Daniel Russell during the election of 1897. Consequently, Russell appointed Young as colonel of the North Carolina Light Infantry Company (NCLI). This historic black militia was largely commissioned for ceremonial functions such as marching in Russell's inaugural parade. However, when duty called in 1898, the NCLI soldiers were among the black troops that participated in the Spanish-American War.[27]

During his travels for ISSA, Shepard encountered a number of African American clergy, many of whom he found ill-suited for their calling and a large number of whom were illiterate. Unlike his father, who was a college-trained minister, a large number of these ministers had no formal education, yet they were "preaching the word of God." Shepard knew the influence that black churches and ministers had in local communities and beyond. Moreover, he thought that the black church would be the institution that could lead the race in the twentieth century. As white southerners continued to embrace Negrophobia and with Washington's philosophy of industrial education becoming the accepted form of black higher education for most white southerners, Shepard finally understood his calling. After traveling extensively for ISSA and experiencing a series of business setbacks, Shepard now wished to move away from the business arena.

He aligned himself with black citizens who believed the best way to advance the race at the dawn of the twentieth century was through education. Shepard wanted to create a school for the proper education of black ministers, since these individuals would be able to go back to their communities to not only discuss theological matters with their congregations but to also train their followers in moral righteousness.

Shepard had finally found a career that would ultimately change his life and the lives of black North Carolinians for generations to come. The route he took to get there was unconventional. He began his professional career as a pharmacist. From there he was co-founder of the NCMPA while garnering a political appointment with the IRS along the way. This journey led him to create a school that would educate black ministers with the hopes that these ministers would ultimately train the masses. In doing so, he sought to make Durham's black community the standard for living out morality in the United States.

2

"Change the Man and the Environments Will Be Changed by Man"

The Creation of the National Religious Training Institution
and Chautauqua for the Negro Race

Let there be no misunderstanding about this, no easy going optimism. We
are not going to share modern civilization just by deserving recognition. We are
going to force ourselves in by organized far-seeing effort-by outthinking and
outflanking the owners of the world today who are too drunk with their own
arrogance and power successfully to oppose us, if we think and learn and do.

W. E. B. Du Bois

On April 22, 1908, James E. Shepard wrote Benjamin Newton Duke in reference
to his ambitions for uplifting his race at the twentieth century's dawn. Shepard
informed the North Carolina businessman that he had two great ambitions,
one of which focused on the creation of "a great university for my people." The
young leader was undoubtedly aware of the financial contributions that the
Duke family made to Trinity College in Durham. He informed Duke that "what
we need now is a college for the colored people which would stand for the same
high ideals as Trinity College stands among the whites." In 1924 Trinity College
changed its name to Duke University because of the large financial contributions that the Duke family made to the college. In his letter, Shepard informed
B. N. Duke that he understood the role of other black colleges in the country
but believed that "they do not seem to be teaching the heart of the matter,"
which from Shepard's standpoint was moral education. Over forty years had
passed since the first black college was founded for the educational purposes of
the newly freed African Americans. Shepard requested funds for the creation
of yet another private black college, this time in Durham, North Carolina. With
a number of public and private black colleges already in existence in North
Carolina, Shepard's job was to influence philanthropists of both races on the

need for another institution in the South. This chapter focuses on the creation of the so-called Shepard's School while revealing his argument for racial uplift through moral education.[1]

At the end of the Civil War, African Americans throughout the South found themselves facing their newly gained freedoms in various ways. One of the first actions for a number of these former slaves was finding loved ones who had previously been sold to slave owners on different plantations. Another way blacks showed their agency during the Reconstruction Era was by engaging with the political process, either by voting or through holding public office. While these political actions were becoming increasingly common among African Americans during the post-Civil War years, seeking education was another way blacks implemented their freedom during this period. Discussing the importance of education for the newly freed slaves, Booker T. Washington recalled, "It was a whole race trying to go to school. Few were too young, and none too old, to make the attempt to learn." Historian Eric Foner argues that gaining access to education was the chief victory for African Americans during this era. Early forms of education for African Americans became a reality as a number of newly freed slaves were trained by organizations such as the American Missionary Association (AMA) prior to the end of slavery. The AMA also helped to open a number of schools during the post–Civil War years for the freedmen. However, through African Americans' desire to gain education, southern poor whites benefited because whites eventually earned the same opportunity through the creation of public schools throughout the South.[2]

With a desire to provide education for African Americans growing in the late 1800s, most middle-class African Americans wanted to go deeper than merely providing the black community with the "three R's." They aspired to provide an avenue that would elevate African Americans so that they could defy the racial stereotyping that had plagued the black community. The black elite desired to rid assumptions that African Americans were lazy; hypersexed; and, overall, immoral. And so racial strategies among African Americans shifted from politics to education during the Gilded Age.[3]

This shift is attributed to the election of Rutherford B. Hayes to the presidency of the United States. During Hayes's tenure as president, the power that blacks had in the political process decreased almost daily. When Hayes was elected president, he agreed to remove federal troops from the South, which left blacks unprotected from acts of violence to prevent them from voting. Many of the early local and national leaders turned their attention away from politics as the preferred savior of the race to advanced education for African Americans. As black males became increasingly disenfranchised from the late 1880s through the early 1900s, a phenomenon was occurring throughout the South— the erection of a number of public and private black colleges throughout the region. Rather than gamble away all of their power on the political process, black lawmakers of the Reconstruction Era made deals that would guarantee higher education for African Americans in racially separate institutions. Most of these early black leaders wanted a more intelligent voting public that would be able to vote on issues which would prove beneficial for the entire race. With the creation of public and private black colleges, a mass of African Americans who had the ability to think critically was being nurtured at the end of slavery. These newly erected, southern-based public black colleges could not openly promote a liberal arts agenda after Booker T. Washington's Atlanta Cotton States Exposition speech in 1895. This was mainly because many white lawmakers felt Washington and the Tuskegee Model should be the standard that black public higher education should follow. This model would make a "better Negro, not a smarter one."[4]

As Washington's model for black higher education became the accepted model for southern-based black colleges, a critical philosophical debate over the proper pedagogy for these institutions ensued between individuals who openly supported liberal arts education and those who argued for industrial instruction for the masses of the black community. Washington's ideas of higher education for the majority of his race were based on the curriculum that his mentor, General Samuel Chapman Armstrong, implemented at Hampton Institute. This curriculum focused primarily on industrial training and was created for the masses of the black community who were fewer than thirty years removed from slavery. Privilege and opportunity were the chief reasons for W. E. B. Du Bois's arguments in favor of "classical education." The concept that Du Bois adopted for higher education was centered on Bishop Henry L. Morehouse's idea of the "talented tenth." Morehouse's view of the talented tenth argued for at least 10 percent of the black population to be trained in Protestant values. Then, members of this talented tenth would return to their communities to educate their neighbors in these values, with the ultimate goal being to subdue the desire for an African American revolt against white Americans. Du Bois furthered this idea by arguing that an advantaged 10 percent of the black community should receive liberal arts training and return to their community as leaders; hence, an elite group of African Americans should receive a liberal arts based higher education so they could effectively serve as the leaders of their race.[5]

The division in the intellectual arena centered on which strategy was best suited for the advancement of the race—Washington's vocational model or Du Bois's talented tenth-classical education concept. These two arguments appear similar in their attempts to uplift their race through higher education. However, the arguments are aimed at two different audiences, with Washington focusing on the masses of the black community and Du Bois speaking of the need for advanced education for the elite. The conflict appeared when these two educators became entangled in a discourse over which form of education would elevate the race at the most rapid pace.[6]

With the Washington–Du Bois debate drawing clear battle lines, many local black leaders had to choose which of these national leaders' philosophies they would support. Choosing sides was especially difficult for local leaders who had ties to education because of Washington's influence in that field. Those who openly opposed Washington and his educational practices would ultimately have to find a new field of work as either Washington or his supporters would force these individuals out of education altogether or see to it that their institutions did not receive sufficient funding. Therefore, many of these early leaders employed tactful approaches when they founded their institutions and incorporated both industrial *and* classical courses in their curricula.[7]

When James Shepard decided to create an educational institution that would benefit African Americans throughout the state of North Carolina, he remained neutral in the Washington–Du Bois debate. According to one of his early biographers, Shepard, through his work with the International Sunday School Association (ISSA), began to realize that African American ministers were largely unqualified to instruct Sunday schools. He wanted to create an institution that would properly train religious leaders and teachers and prepare them to educate the masses. His first objective, however, was to influence prominent black and white philanthropists to support his school. Consequently, with the help of his board of directors, Shepard created a bulletin that revealed the vision of his institution. The first thing that the future president placed on this flyer was the name of the new school, which at the time was the National Training School and Chautauqua for the Colored Race. The naming of black colleges during the early twentieth century was very important as the titles quickly indicated the purpose of these institutions. For example, the designation "Agricultural and Mechanical" (A&M) was added to a number of black colleges during the late 1890s as a result of the second Morrill Act's passage. This law provided federal funds that were extended to southern regions in the 1890s, granting thirty thousand acres of land per the numbers of US representatives in Congress. Proceeds from these land sales could be used only to establish colleges in engineering, agriculture, and military sciences. Many black colleges that used the A&M title in the late nineteenth and early twentieth centuries did not, however, focus primarily on engineering, agriculture, or military sciences. Most were normal schools; therefore, their true titles should have been State Teachers College. On the surface, the name for Shepard's school appeared nonthreatening, with the words "Training School" embedded in the title to suggest that this institution was providing only rudimentary instruction for black students.[8]

This bulletin also made Shepard's case for the creation of another black college in the South, particularly in the state of North Carolina. Shepard and his board of trustees posed and answered a number of concerns that potential donors may have had pertaining to supporting such an institution. For example, one query that was advanced in this circular was "Do the Colored People Need Such an Institution?" Shepard and his committee tackled this question directly by stating that industrial or classical education that "causes the advancement of the real conditions for the race must be [created] upon a moral and religious [base]." Shepard stated that the job of his institution would be to "Change the man and the environments will be changed by the man." It is clear that Shepard and his advisors understood the current theme in the United States, which was the "civilizing mission," an idea that related to the concept of imperialism during the turn of the twentieth century. In the case of black Americans at that time, this concept was linked to the civilizing mission in which American leaders such as President Theodore Roosevelt were responding to Rudyard Kipling's charge in his poem "The White Man's Burden." His argument of "changing the man" was aimed at debunking negative stereotypes of African Americans in the early twentieth century through "moral education."[9]

While he obviously wanted to influence benefactors of both races to support his institution, Shepard also received—and on occasion published—endorsements from high profile leaders in the United States. One of his first endorsements came from President Theodore Roosevelt's vice president, Charles W. Fairbanks, on January 29, 1908. "I fully agree with you that The Sunday School furnishes the most hopeful field for the future work in the uplift of the Negro," the vice president recalled. Obviously, Shepard had forwarded correspondences to the White House pertaining to the need for educating African American ministers, of whom he felt that more than thirty thousand were ill-equipped to properly conduct Sunday school classes because they were illiterate. Echoing Shepard's sentiments of the need to properly train black ministers, Fairbanks closed his endorsement by proclaiming that "th[is] work is worthy of the utmost encouragement."[10]

One of Shepard's most important endorsements came from President Roosevelt himself. On December 18, 1908, Roosevelt informed Shepard that his desire to create a religious training institute was "an admirable one, as you intend to supplement the industrial and higher education of your people by a special religious training." The president ended his letter by proclaiming that "religion and work must go hand in hand, and that your undertakings as presented . . . [are] most commendable." Shepard likely secured these two endorsements due to his work in the Roosevelt administration as deputy collector of the US Internal Revenue Service along with his influence in the national Republican Party. Various governors throughout the South, including Governors Robert B. Glenn, Edmund F. Noel, and Braxton B. Comer of North Carolina, Mississippi, and Alabama, respectively, concurred with the president and vice president in their support of Shepard's school.[11]

While James Shepard continued to build relationships with potential investors in his future school, he also hoped to solidify a bond with the Duke family that was created during his early years in Durham. The individual that Shepard preferred to build a connection with was Benjamin Newton Duke, the chief philanthropist for the Duke family. Ben Duke was the son of Washington Duke, the tobacco tycoon of Durham, North Carolina, and vice president of W. Duke, Sons and Company. When Washington and Benjamin Duke began their philanthropy in the late 1890s, critics such as John R. Webster, in his weekly newspaper in Reidsville, North Carolina, "charged that the philanthropy of the Dukes represented nothing more than an attempt to buy off" or silence an aroused public. Charges of this sort were spurred on because of James Buchanan Duke's vision for moving the Duke family company forward. Ben's brother, James, wanted to market and sell cigarettes during the early 1880s, which caused his father Washington grief from the "moral community."[12]

James Duke aspired to shift W. Duke, Sons and Company from merely being a tobacco company to being a more profitable cigarette business, but the era in which he lived provided great challenges for such a venture. During the Gilded Age, cigarettes were viewed as immoral. They were popularly referred to as dope sticks, devil's toothpicks, little white devils, Satan sticks, joy pills, coffin pills, or coffin nails. Notwithstanding the social stigmas tied to cigarettes, James Duke, through his marketing genius and congressional legislation that lowered the cigarette tax from $1.75 per thousand to $0.50 per thousand, was able to make the family's firm one of the strongest tobacco companies in the world.[13]

Due to a combination of wealth and a backlash against the mass production of cigarettes, the family decided to become major philanthropists in North Carolina. A major amount of the family's donations resulted from Washington Duke's ties to the Methodist Church. Church doctrine called for wealthy parishioners to manage their funds wisely and also to help the downtrodden. Importantly, all of the Dukes were members of the Methodist Church, with Washington Duke serving as a steward of the Trinity Methodist Church in Durham. There also appears to have been a strong connection to the city of Durham, where the entire Duke family, with the exception of James, married, lived, and reared their children. The family had a strong desire to see the city of Durham blossom into a sprawling southern metropolis.[14]

Philanthropic support from the Duke family went not only to the Methodist Church but to other organizations and a number of individuals. African Americans received financial contributions from the Dukes largely as a result of the latter's' political affiliation. According to Duke family historian Robert Durden, the Dukes were Republicans after the Civil War and were viewed as scalawags by some southern Democrats. Of course, a large number of African Americans during the Reconstruction Era were Republicans and therefore were viewed as political allies of the Dukes. With Shepard's connections in the state and national Republican Party, the Duke family probably felt comfortable in at least hearing his appeals for funds.[15]

By 1908 Shepard had begun a capital campaign of sorts aimed solely at the Duke family. He was well aware of their gifts to the black community of North Carolina, which included the building of Durham's Lincoln Memorial Hospital in 1901. Therefore, on October 3, 1908, he wrote Ben Duke, reminding the tobacco tycoon that "you are somewhat acquainted with the great plan for a religious institution devoted to the uplift of the colored race." Remembering that he had already received a number of financial gifts from the Duke family (some were loans that he was delinquent in reimbursing), the young man tactically sidestepped a request for funds. "I promised not to ask you for money soon," he noted, knowing that B. N. Duke likely would not answer another monetary request from Shepard at that time. Therefore, he asked Duke to "donate the land at any place most convenient to you for the sole purpose of a school, and give it [in] honor of your lamented father, who desired to help our race in every possible manner." As became customary for Shepard, he ended this request with a question that on occasion appeared hard for many investors to turn down. In this instance, Shepard concluded by asking, "will you not consider" giving to our institution?[16]

Like his father before him, Shepard understood the importance of face-to-face meetings with large donors. Therefore, during his travels to northern cities, the young educator frequently made "unplanned" visits to the residencies of his benefactors. One such visit occurred in March 1909 while he was visiting Washington, DC. Shepard traveled by train to New York City to have a face-to-face meeting with B. N. Duke, unbeknownst to the philanthropist. En route from the nation's capital, Shepard penned a note to Duke that he would deliver upon arriving in New York in reference to his "surprise" visit. In this letter the educator wrote Duke, "I desire to ask will you grant me five minutes of your time between now and midnight?" Shepard informed this potentially large benefactor of the purpose of the conference with him, which was to discuss the creation of Shepard's school in Durham. He reminded Duke of his desire to see the city of Durham blossom by recalling that "as you are trying so hard to build up Durham, and make it substantial along all lines, I know of nothing that will be a greater monument to you or prove more helpful to a struggling people."[17]

Shepard became a master of appealing for support for his institution by using the ideals of the donors to his advantage. Knowing the love and respect that B. N. Duke had for his father, Washington Duke, and his desire to have the Duke name remembered for generations to come, Shepard informed his potential donor that "what I desire to see you about is to ask you in the event the school is located at Durham, will you erect an auditorium or dormitory to be named after you or your lamented father."[18]

As the spring breezes of 1909 began to fade to the dog days of summer, Shepard's vision of an institution that would "change the man" was beginning to take form. He did not attempt to tackle this enormous task alone but rather surrounded himself with some of the brightest minds in education and business in North Carolina. For example, the first board of advisors of the NRTIC was chaired by James Benson Dudley, the then-president of North Carolina Agricultural and Mechanical College, located in Greensboro, North Carolina (the present-day North Carolina Agricultural and Technical State University). The selection of Dudley as the chair of the advisory committee reveals the respect Shepard had for the A&M college's president, while also expressing the desire that both Dudley and Shepard had for educating African Americans in North Carolina. The respect given both of these individuals by political leaders in the state of North Carolina was revealed years later during the Great Depression, when the state sought to merge the A&M College with North Carolina College for Negroes to save the state money. However, due to the leadership abilities of both Shepard and Dudley, state leaders decided to leave the schools as separate entities and allow these individuals to run their own institutions.[19]

Shepard's board of trustees revealed his wide range of connections. Two of the original trustees for Shepard's School had legal backgrounds. They were Judges N. B. Broughton of Raleigh, North Carolina, and Jeter. C. Pritchard of Asheville, North Carolina (former US senator and associate justice of the Supreme Court of the District of Columbia, 1903–1904). Judge Pritchard became a chief ally of Shepard during the early years of the NRTIC as he used his campaign skills to gain support for the funding of the school.[20]

The institution's focus being on the training of black ministers, the NRTIC had a number of scholars and religious leaders on the board, including Rabbi Abram Simon of Washington, DC; Dr. M. C. B. Mason, a Methodist minister from Cincinnati, Ohio; and Rev. Thomas B. Shannon, a minister from Newark, New Jersey. While the spiritual and legal components of the institution had strong advisors from outside of Durham, the majority of Shepard's business mentors were locals. For example, Dr. Aaron Moore, Julian S. Carr, and John Merrick were all from Durham. Moore and Merrick served as co-founders of the North Carolina Mutual and Provident Association while Carr served as president of the Blackwell's Durham Tobacco Company.[21]

Likely the most intriguing name on this list of advisors was North Carolina Democratic senator Lee S. Overman, the individual who succeeded Judge Jeter C. Pritchard as US senator from North Carolina. This choice was important because Shepard, a registered Republican, openly supported the Republican Party. Moreover, Overman's policies were very conservative and staunchly opposed to the Nineteenth Amendment, which gave women the right to vote. Glenda E. Gilmore argues that most southern politicians who were opposed to the Nineteenth Amendment were afraid that if white women gained the right to vote, ultimately African Americans would regain their franchise in the South. Therefore, they opposed this measure. Notwithstanding his political views, Overman served as an original trustee for Shepard's School, showing Shepard's wide range of political connections within both parties in the South.[22]

With a strong board of advisors in place, Shepard began a capital campaign to fund his new institution. As the Duke family's philanthropy continued, Shepard began to fine-tune his appeal for funds for what he perceived as the "Negro" version of Trinity College. On September 22, 1909, the NRTIC administrator penned a letter to B. N. Duke, this time requesting a meeting that would lead to others donating to his school. In this note, Shepard praised Duke for a recent gift that he had given to Trinity, proclaiming that "you are always doing big things and will live forever in the hearts of those whom this Institution has influenced and benefited." In an attempt to sidestep making a direct request for a financial contribution from Duke, Shepard informed the tobacco tycoon that "I understand your attitude towards the work in which I am interested and I shall not ask you for money." Not allowing Duke off the hook, the president's plea for a face-to-face meeting became more aggressive as Shepard informed the Duke's family agent for philanthropy that "somehow I am more than anxious to have a frank ten minute talk with you and seek your advice and suggestion" as it pertains to the creation of the NRTIC.[23]

During the fall of 1909, Shepard and his advisors traveled throughout the nation and wrote to a number of local and national philanthropists from whom he wanted support. For example, in one of his appeals for funds to James Sprunt of Wilmington, North Carolina, Shepard introduced his idea of the NRTIC as a place that would "be of no particular creed, but open to all faiths, and is designed especially to meet the needs of the leadership of the race." ("All faiths" presumably meant all Protestant faiths.) The NRTIC president informed this donor of the need of educating black ministers throughout the South by explaining that "we have 30,000 colored ministers in the United States, and a safe estimate is that only ten percent of them are educated; [therefore,] we have an unintelligent leadership." Those were the individuals his institution desired to educate. Moreover, he argued that the work in creating this institution would appeal to "every lover of humanity, and especially those interested in the uplift of the colored race." Not desiring to miss an opportunity to request funds, Shepard informed this potential benefactor of a recent meeting with his advisors where they expressed the need for $5,000 before they could begin construction of an auditorium for his school. Along with this request, the administrator provided a list of prominent individuals who endorsed the creation of the NRTIC and with whom Sprunt was surely familiar. These supporters lived as far away as New York City and as near as Winston-Salem, North Carolina. Shortly thereafter, Sprunt became a donor whom Shepard would contact whenever his institution was in need of funds.[24]

Advising Shepard on the creation of his school was just one role of his board of advisors. They also "stomped" for funds on behalf of Shepard and the NRTIC. For example, on October 14, 1909, just over three months after the NRTIC was incorporated, Shepard and his trustees met to advance the cause of his institution. After that meeting, these consultants returned to their homes and raised "cash and pledges over $19,000." This call to action was in response to the board's desire to wage "an aggressive campaign . . . to secure $21,000 additional within the next 90 days" for the erection of an auditorium. According to Shepard, his advisors "believe that this is the most far reaching scheme ever attempted for the uplift of the race." "It is unique," Shepard noticed. Nevertheless, fund-raising for the NRTIC was only a portion of what Shepard and his advisors desired for the school. They also wanted "to gather in the leadership of the race and try to change and train them" so they could change the environments in which they lived.[25]

With the emergence of a new year, Shepard began to refocus on his relationship with B. N. Duke, this time revealing the true curriculum of his school. Just nineteen days into the year of 1910, Shepard wrote yet another letter to Duke, informing the philanthropist of his desire to open the doors of his institution during the summer of 1910. Once again arguing for the need of an educated group of black ministers, Shepard recalled that "First, Religious and Moral instruction for the leaders of the race" will be provided at this institution. His school would "bring these leaders together for instruction by the best minds, white and colored, and send them out to train others." Shepard desired to train these ministers in classical education with the hope that once trained, these leaders would return to their communities to educate their neighbors, thus incorporating the Morehouse–Du Bois model of higher education. Therefore, the education that these newly trained ministers received from the NRTIC moved beyond the basic literacy and vocational instruction. This curriculum incorporated the ideas of some of the greatest academic minds of the day, such as those of scholars Kelly Miller and W. E. B. Du Bois. Thus, this training went far beyond teaching illiterate ministers how to read. Instead, the NRTIC's true mission was to create black moral leaders who had the ability to think critically and therefore serve as the true leaders of their race.[26]

Shepard also understood the educational atmosphere that he was entering, which was predominantly formed by the president of the Tuskegee Institute, Booker T. Washington. Shepard informed Duke of his desire to infuse forms of industrial education in his school's course of study. For example, Shepard recalled that a "plan to gather the city and country school teachers to give lessons in industrial . . . , home gardening, horticulture, sewing and cooking, agriculture and to show that these things are practical in every walk of life." Shepard was making strong attempts to fuse both the classical and vocational forms of education in his school because he felt that "work and religion should go hand in hand." Ending this particular note to Duke, Shepard informed his potential investor that this "investment will pay in the large number of people reached and helped." For the first time, Shepard was placing in writing his full platform before a benefactor. Despite the letter, B. N. Duke appeared somewhat reluctant to support the idea of the NRTIC in a more generously manner. This hesitation was likely due to Shepard's less than stellar past in terms of his experience in business finance.[27]

Just a few weeks later, Shepard fired off another appeal for funds to B. N. Duke, this time on Valentine's Day of 1910. As usual, noticing the influence that Duke had in funding Trinity College, Shepard informed this philanthropist, "I know that you have made Trinity, perhaps the greatest Institution in the South." Shepard informed Ben that his brother, James Duke, earlier to his correspondence with Ben, had a conversation with former congressman Cheatham about the creation of the NRTIC. Shepard advised Ben that his brother "promised to take up the matter with you, and treat us right." Apparently, the "president-elect" of the NRTIC felt that if he had the support of J. B. Duke, then Ben would begin to fund this institution on levels like his support of Trinity College.[28]

Early in his appeals to Duke, Shepard sought to establish a correlation between the NRTIC and Trinity College because he understood the role that B. N. Duke and his family played in creating the foundation for the latter institution. The early histories of Trinity and the NRTIC share similarities, as Trinity was originally known as the Union Institute and founded by Quakers and Methodists in the 1830s. After going through a series of phases such as "including a state-supported emphasis in the 1850s on the training of school teachers," the institution was eventually adopted by the Methodist Church of North Carolina in 1856 and took the name of Trinity College in 1859. Located in Randolph County, North Carolina, just seventy miles west of Durham in 1887, and facing bankruptcy, Ben Duke gave the college $1,000 to stabilize the impoverished institution. According to historian Robert Durden, the Duke family was proud of Trinity's "service to 'poor boys' who could pay little and most of whom tended to become preachers and teachers." Moreover, B. N. Duke was a vital leader in the moving of Trinity College from Randolph County to Durham; he served as the de facto chair of the building committee (his father Washington was the de jure chair at seventy years old), and for several years he was a trustee of that institution.[29]

Yet Ben Duke remained hesitant to support the creation of another black college in the state of North Carolina. In the face of this, Shepard insisted that "this school is different from any now established." In an attempt to define the different mission of his school from that of other black colleges in the South, he wrote that "it conflicts with none, and fills a unique place in racial uplift." The new educator argued that "men and women will be taught that practical religion means practical work, and we are going to try and build up in Durham and elsewhere a type of Negro citizen of whom you will be proud." Trying to encourage good race relations in their city and state through the graduates of Shepard's school, the latter recalled that "the friendliness of the white people of Durham makes it the ideal place." The level of development in the city and the fact that there was no black college in Durham also played deciding factors in his plan. Shepard ended his note in a manner that played on his religious background, while once again incorporating Trinity College in his final push. The president closed by stating that "I do not believe that anything would please God more than to see in one end of town, a monument to the white race, and in the other, a monument to the struggling black race, both seeking to point men to him." While many may have ended this note at that point, Shepard went on to close this correspondence with his usual request: "Will you not help us?"[30]

By the summer of 1910, the creation of the NRTIC was moving full steam ahead. For example, on July 23 of that year, Horace D. Scatter of the *Chicago Defender* published an article on the school, which opened its summer program on July 10, 1910, by proclaiming that "North Carolina is Awakening." In this essay, Scatter argued that the school had been opened for two weeks and was a greater success than anyone imagined. By the second week, the school had reached numbers nearing one hundred, made up primarily of teachers, preachers, and "others from varied walks of life among the Negroes." The course of study was described as "normal and primary methods, history, geography, grammar, pedagogy, domestic science, dressmaking and millinery, basketry and vocal music." This curriculum reveals Shepard's desire to incorporate both the classical and vocational forms of higher education.[31]

During the first summer of this school, Shepard invited a series of lecturers, including the Reverend Jesse Hurburt, of Newark, New Jersey, who lectured the students on Bible instruction and was followed by the Reverend Dr. W. Y. Chapman. Although Bible instruction was an important factor in the NRTIC's curriculum, other forms of classical education were also promoted during the opening weeks of Shepard's School. For example, Miss Grace Hemmingway, "the well known child story teller," instructed the students on the art of storytelling. The remaining lecturers for that summer included Samuel J. McCraken, Judge N. B. Broughton, and Bishop George Wylie Clinton. From all accounts, the first six-week summer session of the NRTIC was successful as the number of students doubled at its opening that fall. In reference to the good deeds of Dr. Shepard and his school, Bishop Robert Strange of the Eastern North Carolina

Dioceses recalled that "I think highly of Dr. Shepard, and I believe this institution will be a real help to the Negro."[32]

With his institution now open and initially successful, Shepard's dream of a school that would "change the man" had finally come to fruition. Now his task was to make sure that the doors of the institution remained open for those who desired to acquire the training that his school provided. As Shepard and the NRTIC began to take root in Durham, a number of obstacles persisted regarding the long-term financial maintenance of the school. Nevertheless, his overall desire to help uplift the race through "changing the man" had led the president to hire an "intelligent" faculty that would help separate his students from others who attended black colleges throughout the South. Although the days ahead appeared brighter, challenges regarding the long-term health of the college loomed on the horizon. Shepard, nonetheless, had finally reached a milestone in his life by opening the NRTIC with the hope that this institution would "advance the race" in the twentieth century.

3

Creating an Intellectual Partnership While Easing the White Man's Burden

James E. Shepard Advancing the Race through His Intellectual
Partnerships

Whenever one goes into a community he will find that every negro has a
white friend and every white man has one negro that he absolutely trusts and
depends on. Whenever a negro gets into trouble in any community, he goes to a
white man who helps him out of trouble, in fact, the average negro . . . keeps his
white man picked out to use in troublesome times.

Booker T. Washington

To be president of a college and white is no bed of roses. To be president
of a college and black is almost a bed of thorns.

Benjamin E. Mays

During the autumn of 1910, and one year after the opening of James Shepard's National Religious Training Institute and Chautauqua for the Negro Race
(NRTIC), the preeminent "Negro educator," Booker T. Washington, embarked
on an Educational Tour of the state of North Carolina in which he attempted
to place "Black progress on display." According to writer William Henry Lewis,
Washington's visit to this southern state was "improving the condition of his
own race and bringing about more friendly relations between the two races."
Importantly, Washington and Shepard shared similar strategies in terms of
racial uplift during the early twentieth century. Both of these individuals were
presidents of southern "Negro colleges" and both also desired to create industrious, moral citizens. Therefore, with the formation of these institutions, one
primarily focusing on industrial education (Tuskegee, founded in 1881) and
another establishing moral instruction through liberal arts education (NRTIC,
founded in 1910), the southern Negro would not only have a group of citizens

that could build their own communities; they would also have "moral citizens" properly trained to lead them.[1]

On his tour, Washington traveled with the most prominent black citizens of the Tar Heel State with the desire to display their accomplishments for the world to see. During this time frame, negative stereotypes of African Americans were the rule of the day, and therefore Washington wanted to dispel these myths by parading the most prominent African American citizens for both the white and black communities to witness. For example, on stops in major cities of North Carolina, the Wizard of Tuskegee allowed many of these prominent blacks the opportunity to give brief speeches before the audiences leading up to his key-note address. Importantly, on the Tuskegee man's visit to the city of Durham, James E. Shepard introduced Washington to a half-black and half-white crowd of that city. Shepard was likely chosen to give the introduction of Washington over Charles C. Spaulding and other prominent black Durhamites because of the connection that Shepard and Washington shared. Such associations as their political connection with the national Republican Party and the trust that Washington had in Shepard's integrity likely pushed his name over that of Spaulding's. Opportunities such as introducing Booker T. Washington before one of his speeches eventually placed James Shepard in the same company as some of the most prominent black educators of his day. Therefore, he was able to create a number of intellectual partnerships that would help advance the mission of the NRTIC, thus helping to uplift his race in the state of North Carolina.[2]

During the infancy of the NRTIC, President Shepard continued to display his ability to make connections with the most prominent citizens of both races in the South. With these relationships in hand, Shepard was able to advance the ideals of his institution while being strapped for cash. Notwithstanding the difficulties in financing his school, Shepard was able to create a number of intellectual partnerships that benefited the NRTIC while also helping to "uplift the race" by incorporating Washington's philosophy of "placing black progress on display." Nevertheless, this chapter will argue that through Shepard's intellectual partnerships, the NRTIC attempted to advance the race by debunking negative stereotypes of the Negro during the early twentieth century. Moreover, these partners were not only instructing Shepard's students on the proper way of becoming "moral citizens," they were also strategizing for the black community, a group less than fifty years removed from the horrors of slavery.

The idea of a black college inculcating its pupils with moral instruction was not unique to James Shepard and the NRTIC during the early twentieth century. The vast majority of these institutions were preaching morality to their students during the "nadir of the black experience" as a means of racial uplift through the civilizing mission. Moreover, most of the northern donors to black education during the late nineteen and early twentieth centuries argued that "industrial education imbued with moral dictates, served as a form of social control." Nevertheless, for privately funded black colleges that wanted to gain support from northern educational benevolent societies such as the General Education Board (GEB), Julius Rosenwald Fund, and Anna T. Jeanes Funds, they not only had to incorporate industrial education but also infuse "moral training" in their curriculum in order to give the illusion that their white benefactors were helping to shape not only black education at the turn of the century but the black community as a whole.[3]

Importantly for James Shepard, however, his aims did not focus on infusing morality with industrial education, but rather on liberal arts instruction with a heavy dose of moral inculcation. Therefore, when he approached the GEB for funds in the creation of his institution with no mention of industrial training, the board members responded that the "plan of the institution set forth in the prospectus embrace[s] a college or university on the one hand, and a Chautauqua or training school on the other." In a stronger sign of disapproval of Shepard's desire to create such an institution, while also displaying their ability to see through the naming of his school as being merely "instructional" and rating the institution on the merit of the curriculum, the GEB argued that the three departments that the NRTIC proposed to operate included "a literary department, a theological department, and a commercial department." Due to his lack of focus on industrial education, the GEB denied Shepard's request for funds despite his attempts to infuse the idea of the civilizing mission.[4]

While "moral instruction" played an integral role in the funding of black colleges during the late nineteenth and early twentieth centuries, it was not exclusive to black colleges during that time. For example, Predominantly White Colleges and Universities (PWCUs) presidents during this era believed their mission was to "enhance the reputations of campuses [while] inspire[ing] the development of character and education for generations of students." Moreover, during this period a number of PWCU presidents were "preacher/presidents" hoping that their training would not only enlighten their students in the fields of academia, but also on the proper ways to lead morally righteous lives.[5]

Nevertheless, while morality and educational instruction went hand-in-hand during the Progressive Era, there was some doubt about black college administrators' ability to give their students proper instruction. For example, B. C. Caldwell, a white field secretary of the Jeanes and Slater Funds, viewed black colleges operated by African American administrators as weak. Caldwell recalled in a report that schools which were entirely controlled by African Americans were "marked by detachment, isolation" and argued that black religious leaders who delved into education were "autocrats with no more religion than the law allows." Moreover, Caldwell and a number of other white southerners believed that black education should be led by white individuals who held the best interest for the black community. Therefore, black college presidents such as Booker T. Washington of Alabama, William J. Hale of Tennessee, John Hope of Georgia, Nathan B. Young of Florida, and James E. Shepard of North Carolina were all aware of the environment in which they operated. Therefore, these black college presidents and others displayed their desire to "ease the white man's burden" by inculcating their students with spiritual morality through their different curricula (either liberal arts or industrial education) while also infusing the idea of race consciousness among their students.[6]

With Washington's educational tour of North Carolina in 1910 and the issue of who could properly lead a black college in the early twentieth century serving as his backdrop, James Shepard's role as president of the NRTIC reveals his ability to make connections with the most prominent citizens of both races of the South. With the arrival of a new year, and President Shepard's goal of creating an institution that would "change the man" fulfilled, the need for appropriations for his school grew stronger daily. Nevertheless, his continued efforts to gain support from Benjamin Newton Duke eventually paid off. On February 8, 1911, the college administrator wrote the philanthropist thanking him for a gift of five hundred dollars that would be used to further Shepard's desire to "uplift the race" through moral instruction. Shepard informed Duke that these funds would help to "erect a building for the training of young colored women as settlement workers, Y.M.C.A. secretaries, organizers of neighborhood societies; to teach them household economics, dietetics, sanitation and, in fact, to train a class of mothers who will produce a higher and better type of citizen." Here the president is attacking the idea of the "white man's burden" by revealing that his school would instruct young women on the proper ways to become productive citizens in the United States, while also revealing that these young women would return to their communities and instruct their neighbors in the ways of their NRTIC training.[7]

While Dr. Shepard continued to lobby B. N. Duke for funds for his school, the summer session of 1911 gave Shepard an opportunity to discuss the aims of his institution, such as the aim of instructing his pupils on the role that religion should play in the black community. "If a man's religion be founded and based on the right ideas," the president recalled, "he will be industrious, thrifty and honest and of his own accord will do what is right and just." While "good Christian character" was a major theme in Shepard's address to the media and philanthropists, a heavy dose of liberal arts training was provided to his students by some of the best-known scholars in the South as well as the nation. Ironically, Shepard's school was spared attack from white conservatives for being radical because Shepard and his advisors argued that his school was "changing the man" and therefore creating good Christians. While many other black colleges that were founded during this same era had to openly display a vocational education curriculum, Shepard only had to prove to his donors that his institution was providing an education that would train African Americans to become better citizens morally. Therefore, the NRTIC was able to openly display their desire to educate their students in the liberal arts because according to Shepard, "The school trains the leaders and the leaders go among the people to teach them"; thus, this institution would eventually "ease the white man's burden."[8]

While the major focus of his school early on was on providing proper instruction for black ministers, President Shepard saw the need for a conference for Negro pastors to take place during the summer of 1912. The idea for such a conference came about as a consequence of the success of the 1911 summer session of Shepard's school in which hundreds of ministers attended. During that session, ministers of both races were instructed by leading theologians and secular scholars in an attempt to broaden these individuals' academic knowledge. Some of the well-known lecturers were the president of Trinity College (later Duke University), Bishop John C. Kilgo, and Professor Kelly Miller of Howard University.[9]

Word of Shepard's success in training ministers during the summer of 1911 spread like wildfire; therefore, he was quickly charged with conducting a conference for African American pastors, which would include ministers from all over the nation. Proudly answering this call, the president issued a statement in support of the convention, which would be held at the NRTIC, by proclaiming, "This conference is for the purpose of discussing the moral, civil, and spiritual condition of the Negro." Shepard concluded his announcement by enthusiastically asserting that this conference for black pastors would work "along practical lines for the uplift of the race, especially through religious channels." For Shepard, a meeting of this sort proved to be a bonus, as it helped to expand his agenda of uplifting his race through the proper training of "Negro" ministers who, he argued, were the moral leaders of the community. In addition, this conference would be held at his school, which would provide national exposure to this young institution, thus helping his effort in fund-raising. Moreover, with the presence of black ministers from around the nation on his campus for training, Shepard would have the opportunity to broaden the walls of the NRTIC from the corners of Durham to areas in the country that likely had little to no knowledge of the existence of his school. Here, Shepard's and the NRTIC's star began to rise quickly, although he was still building the school's financial and physical infrastructure.[10]

Shortly after the announcement of the Conference for Negro Pastors, which was scheduled to be held during the summer of 1912, the second full academic year of Shepard's school commenced. George King of the *Pittsburgh Courier* proclaimed in a headline on November 18, 1911 that a "New Awakening in Education" was occurring at Shepard's Chautauqua. According to early reports, the president's message of "changing the man" went international. During the second academic year of the NRTIC, two foreign students, one from Africa and one from India, enrolled for instruction in his school. Aside from these two international students, the NRTIC's second year was almost filled to capacity with both local and national African American pupils of both genders.[11]

With such a quick increase in the student population, the young administrator had to grapple with the idea of the quality of education these individuals would obtain. Therefore, Shepard created an intellectual partnership "with a faculty composed of teachers from the leading institutions of the country," according to editor George King. One such instructor was Professor C. G. O'Kelly, who served as professor of music for the school in its infancy. Moreover, O'Kelly was considered "one of the most experienced pedagogues the [black race] has." During the first year of Professor O'Kelly's instruction at the NRTIC, the band and orchestra compared "favorably with similar organizations when the age of the school is taken into consideration." It is also significant that his instruction focused on both classical music and "folk songs of the race." Once again, there was no attempt by Shepard or anyone in his administration to hide the fact that they employed an individual who trained his students in classical music. This lack of concealment can be attributed to the fact that this form of instruction would expose these students to Western mainstream values, thus keeping with the idea of the "civilizing mission."[12]

Also, neither the NRTIC nor Shepard was attacked by Booker T. Washington or any of his Bookerites for not providing a proper education for African Americans during the nadir of the black experience. This tacit quiet support can best be attributed to a number of factors: first, Shepard's pedagogy was not challenging Washington's Tuskegee model in any way. As previously seen, both Washington and Shepard subscribed to the "civilizing mission" in terms of "racial uplift;" therefore, they were fighting the same battle. Second, it is clear that

Shepard, Washington, and a vast number of black college presidents of this era understood the need for vocational education, classical education, and "moral instruction." Thus, there was no competition between Washington and Shepard as both desired to advance the race through the philosophies they incorporated at their institutions of higher education.[13]

While Shepard's school was gaining traction during its infancy, cases of violence against African Americans were also peaking during this time. The issue of racial violence was a chief concern faced by all southern black college presidents during the Jim Crow Era. Moreover, black men were being lynched on the basis of false claims of raping a white "lady" and of failures to adhere to the social customs of the Jim Crow era, such as removing hats for whites, stepping off of sidewalks for whites, and the reckless eyeballing of white women. Many of the early black college presidents understood that they were community leaders; however, they also knew that their first priority was the protection of their institutions. Therefore, on the surface, many of these individuals remained silent when such harsh violations of human rights occurred in the black community. Importantly, many of these presidents, while outwardly silent, led behind-the-scenes efforts against such activities. For example, as early as December 2, 1911, James Shepard wrote the editor of the *Charlotte Observer*, John C. Hemphill, to express his appreciation for an article that devastatingly denounced lynchings.[14]

In this correspondence, Shepard thanked Hemphill for "one of the boldest, manliest, and fairest articles" on lynching to date. The president argued in this note that the black community was not an immoral one and that through his institution and the black church they were becoming more moral. Shortly thereafter, Shepard's tone in this correspondence suddenly changed. The president assured the editor that "the Negroes who are striving for better things are seeking to put down crime, to obey law and to promote that feeling of friendship and peace" which many blacks wished for during the Jim Crow Era. Recalling his fund-raising speeches in the North that attempted to paint the South as a pleasant place for African Americans, Shepard informed Hemphill of his views on race relations in the South. "The southern people at heart are the real friends of the Negro," Shepard proclaimed, and "they understand him better and there is coming to be more and more . . . sympathetic feeling between the best of both races." Highlighting the "conservative" spirit of the people of North Carolina, the president reminded Hemphill of the creditable fact that North Carolina was without a "reported lynching" for the past "three or four years," which he attributed to the "spirit of helpfulness that has always characterized the citizens of North Carolina."[15]

Ironically, while the president penned this letter to Hemphill, racial violence in the United States during the years from 1900 through 1920 was at the highest level recorded in American history; nevertheless, Shepard desired to paint a picture of racial harmony in North Carolina to curry favor from progressive-minded white southerners who could lend support to his school. Therefore, this letter appears to have been written by Shepard to help promote his institution rather than as simply expressing his gratitude for Hemphill's article on lynching. For example, after the president forwarded Hemphill this congratulatory letter in response to the editor's overview of the horrors of racial violence in the South, Hemphill received a major promotion by becoming a writer for the *New York Times*. Shortly thereafter, Shepard wrote another note to "his secret ally" in New York wishing him well on his journey. In that letter, however, Shepard appeared to encourage Hemphill to write a line or two about the NRTIC in his new paper to help promote Shepard's cause. In response, Hemphill informed the young administrator that going through another newspaper would perhaps be a better option than the *New York Times*. Therefore, he desired to link Shepard up with Oswald Garrison Villard, the editor of the *New York Evening Post*, "who has always taken a lively interest in such work as you are doing." Ironically, not only was Villard president and editor of the *New York Evening Post*, and grandson of abolitionist William Lloyd Garrison, he was also the individual who issued the call on February 12, 1909, "to all believers in democracy to join a national conference to discuss present evils, the voicing of protests, and the renewal of the struggle for civil and political liberty," thus spearheading the creation of the National Association for the Advancement of Colored People (NAACP). Notwithstanding Villard's appreciation for Shepard's program early on, the college administrator would eventually come into direct conflict with the NAACP as it attempted to integrate the University of North Carolina at Chapel Hill's graduate school in the 1930s with the use of one of his students, which Shepard successfully blocked by simply withholding the student's transcript.[16]

Another editor with whom Hemphill helped Shepard build a relationship was Walter H. Page, editor of *World's Work*, because he also was "very much interested in the mission to which you have devoted your life." Walter Page and James Shepard shared both local and national connections as well, with Page receiving a degree from Trinity College in Durham and later in his career being appointed ambassador to the United Kingdom during World War I by President Woodrow Wilson. Ironically, Wilson, a Democratic president, actually supported Shepard's mission of the NRTIC. According to North Carolina Central University historian Beverly Jones, Shepard's appreciation for newspaper editors can be credited to a position he held in the late 1890s as editor of the *Safe-*

guard newspaper which, according to Jones, was "devoted to the perpetuation of Republican principles." The partnerships that were being created during the infancy of the NRTIC would surely pay off as the president began to dispatch one of his chief associates and school trustee Jeter C. Pritchard to rally financial support for his institution.[17]

Heeding Shepard's request, circuit court judge and NRTIC advisor Jeter C. Pritchard traveled to northern states to gain financial support for Shepard's institution. During the summers of 1911 and 1912 in particular, Pritchard's fundraising led him to northern areas, where his connections would be better served. During his 1912 tour, for example, the *Pittsburgh Courier* headlined an article "White Judge is Traveling for Negro School: P. C. Pritchard of Ashville, N. C. Working for National Religious School." Obviously George King, the *Courier*'s editor, was not clear on Pritchard's first name, assuming his full name was Peter C. Pritchard. Nevertheless, King was very clear on Pritchard's mission of promoting the NRTIC while gaining support for Shepard's institution.[18]

The judge's first desire on this tour was to express a sense of racial harmony in North Carolina, which he hoped would jump-start support for this privately funded black college. Pritchard argued, "I want to correct the false impression that seems to be very widespread in all sections of the country." The judge was alluding to the heated race relations occurring in the South and in North Carolina particularly. Moreover, the judge proclaimed, "the whites and the colored people in North Carolina are far from being at sword's points. On the contrary, I feel safe in saying that there is as good a feeling between races in North Carolina as in any state in the Union." Clearly this sentiment was a stretch, as the state of North Carolina had just twelve years earlier totally disenfranchised African American male voters through trickery and violence, as was the case in Wilmington, North Carolina, in the late 1890s.[19]

Nevertheless, Pritchard continued this speech by proclaiming, "There is more racial prejudice in the North than in the South, and this can be attributed largely to the fact [that] many of the Negroes who come north are ignorant adventurers who think that they can better themselves in this section of the country without working." Pritchard was speaking to the anxieties that many northern whites had pertaining to an influx of southern African Americans into northern urban areas. This point is best explained by historian Nicholas Lemann, who argues that for the first time in their lives, many white northerners were faced with a large number of black migrants during this era; therefore, they were in search for ways to place borders around themselves that would ultimately segregate the two races in a de facto manner.[20]

Now, with his white, northern audience members on the edge of their chairs listening in approval, Pritchard began to inform these potential donors of James E. Shepard's vision of educating African Americans. "The school which Doctor Shepard has founded is not a denominational one," Pritchard told the crowd while also recalling that Shepard felt that "the people can best be reached through the ministers of their own race." With an attempt to argue for the effectiveness of such an education for African Americans, Pritchard asserted that "the Negro can make a first-class citizen and a patriotic citizen. . . . The man who loves his God loves his country, and it is pretty well proved that the Negro loves his God."[21]

Not forgetting the desire of many southern whites to return the South to the customs of the antebellum era while also attempting to "re-unite" the country in a way that David Blight describes in *Race and Reunion* (2001). Pritchard systematically unraveled his argument of "national unity." The judge did this by stating Shepard's argument that the NRTIC was helping the "Negro" advance himself. In doing so, Pritchard proclaimed that "there was a time when people in the South felt that their interest[s] were entirely separate from the interest[s] of the people of any other section of the country, but now we all feel that it is just as important to the people of Massachusetts to have good citizenship in North Carolina as it is to the people of that state." This cry from Pritchard was surely aimed to rally support from these northern whites in support of their white brothers and sisters in North Carolina to help "ease their burden." To strengthen that point, Shepard's trustee recalled that as a judge he "had names on the criminal docket of every race except one and that was the Jew." Pritchard went on to explain, "I attribute this to the fact that the Jews are more careful in home life and they are more particular in the training of their boys and girls at home." Therefore, from Pritchard's perspective, with the use of the "Jewish model," Shepard's schools would train the Negro in North Carolina to be moral citizens and thus "remove a large part of the evil" that has engulfed the African American community.[22]

To some, Pritchard's message to this white northern audience may have appeared to support the same negative stereotypes of the Negro that Shepard's school desired to debunk; sadly, these are the same tactics that a number of black college administrators had to employ during the nadir of the black experience in order to gain financial support for their institutions. For example, Booker T. Washington often told "darkie jokes" before white audiences that also happened to be potential donors of the Tuskegee Institute. These jokes served multiple purposes: first, to create a sense of comfort for the white philanthropists that were actually witnessing these speeches. Second, to show his crowd how more advanced he was than the individuals he desired to teach, which would ultimately "ease the white man's burden" by educating them in the "civilizing mission" or having them assimilate into American culture.[23]

This argument is important because according to historian Kenneth Goings, affluent whites created a class system for white education that relegated the lower classes of whites to "rudimentary education," while the gentry were afforded the opportunity to receive training in the classics. Nevertheless, black college administrators clearly understood the psychology of upper-class whites in terms of the role they felt black education should follow, which was to create "a better Negro, not a smarter one." Therefore, many African American college presidents during the Jim Crow Era understood that if they wanted to gain support from white donors, they had to agree on the surface with the assumption that the masses of the black population only decades removed from the institution of slavery were immoral, ignorant, and lazy while also revealing their (the black college presidents') desire to rid the black community of such habits. However, their real motive was to eliminate the basis for these stereotypes from the African American community as a whole by training individuals who would carry themselves in a manner that would make it hard for any citizen, white or black, to consider African Americans immoral, ignorant, or lazy. Therefore, a number of Negro colleges during the nadir focused on inculcating their students with Victorian values while also promoting liberal arts, as well as industrial education, in their curriculum.[24]

While Shepard and the NRTIC continued to battle the negative social stigmas that were connected to the black community, the fiscal operations of his institution demanded the president's full attention. Therefore, for the next ten years President Shepard's primary focus centered on the fiscal well-being of his institution. Like many privately funded black colleges during the early years of the Jim Crow Era, Shepard and his advisors faced severe economic challenges that actually threatened the survival of his school. Rather than give in to pressures of this task, however, Shepard—clearly understanding these dire circumstances—quickly shifted into campaign mode. Much of the funds that supported his school during these days came from private donors such as B. N. Duke and from the students' tuition, which at the time was only ten dollars per six-week course, plus an additional three dollars for room and board. Nevertheless, according to Beverly Jones, Shepard refused to assess a fee to ministers who were being trained at his institution as he felt that these individuals were the backbone of the race and, if given a proper education, could effectively lead them. At the same time, Shepard did not dismiss the "regular students" if they did not have the means financially to continue their course work at the institution. To help offset the cost of those students who did not have the full amount of money to enter school, Shepard, like many black college presidents of the early twentieth century, instituted a work-study program. According to Marjorie Shepard, one of James and Annie Shepard's daughters, her father "was able to find some of [the students] odd job[s]—[like] cleaning and yard work—to pay their tuition." Moreover, keeping with the spirit of many black colleges during this era and later ones, Shepard and the NRTIC did not want to turn any student away who displayed the desire and mental ability to learn.[25]

To help ease the financial burdens of his school, Shepard created a partnership with a prominent real estate broker, G. C. Farthing. According to Jones, this partnership became so strong that Shepard's loans from this real estate broker were considered "Shepard notes." The president entered into a relationship with Farthing that would place the realtor into some fiscal hardship. For example, Shepard, with the approval of his board of advisors, "issued bonds up to $100,000 using the school as collateral." According to Jones, "Farthing, [who] believed that the school would ultimately be successful and personally admired Shepard—invested in $50,000 worth of bonds" himself. Sadly for Shepard and his friend, however, his bonds were liquidated due to an "inactive real estate market." It has yet to be ascertained if Farthing held any ill will toward Shepard for the loss of such a substantial investment. Either placing personal feelings aside or desiring not to be projected as a poor investor, the real estate broker stayed above the fray in terms of his lost investment. For example, when Farthing was asked why he did not sell the Shepard's notes, he simply responded: "I believe Shepard is going to strike it big one of these days. I am backing him in that belief."[26]

Prior to the housing market's failure, Shepard issued a series of appeals for funds to one of his benefactors, B. N. Duke. In a note on February 26, 1913, the administrator informed Duke that his school had issued bonds for $75,000, with most going to "Mr. Farthing to secure his indebtedness." Shepard went on to inform Duke that he was going to initiate an aggressive financial campaign for funds that was being supported by "Dr. Booker T. Washington." According to Shepard, Washington supported this action with the "understanding that the Board is to be reorganized" and a local treasurer be put on the grounds to handle the school's money. Much like his time as a pharmacist in the late nineteenth century, Shepard had a difficult time managing the finances of his enterprise (see chapter 1). Unlike his drugstore, Shepard finally understood his calling: to help uplift his race through moral instruction. The curriculum, faculty, staff, and the partnerships that Shepard built while creating this institution eventually would pay off for the overall survival of the school, notwithstanding his inability to appropriately manage the school's funds.[27]

At end of 1914, Dr. Shepard's knowledge of finances was again called into question. This time a local colleague, Dr. William Preston Few, president of Duke University, expressed some concerns pertaining to the matter. Apparently, Shepard reached out to Few for advice in finding funds to help his institution during a time when many donors were holding back due to the emergence of World War I. Few's response was similar to that of Booker T. Washington; however, it was not what the NRTIC president expected, as the Duke president suggested that Shepard employ a "competent auditor" to oversee the fiscal operations of the school before seeking outside funds. The black college president responded to this advice by giving Duke's administrator a quick lecture on the difference between the operations of black colleges and PWCUs during the early twentieth century. "With 150 students and a teaching staff of 12 with no endowment money, an auditor would not help," Shepard argued. Moreover, from the NRTIC's president perspective, creating an auditor's position during that time would only serve as another employee to pay at a time when funds were sorely limited. Moving on in this note that ended up serving as a subdued tongue-lashing to his colleague, Shepard explained, "When students are charged $10.00 per month for room and board and can't pay that sum, an auditor will not help." Here, once again, the NRTIC president was informing Duke's president not only of the different challenges that he faced as being the leader of a black college at that time, but also of the vicissitudes his students faced as well in terms of securing room and board while also not having the financial means to do so.[28]

Lastly, Shepard argued, "To run this plant, it would cost $1600 per month and I can only depend on $600 in cash monthly, an auditor will not help." Therefore, from Shepard's perspective, placing the operational criteria of a PWCU on a black college was grossly outlandish. Also, based on a series of communications between Shepard and Benjamin Duke, Shepard clearly understood that he had made mistakes in terms of the financial operations of his institution; however, he also felt that his school was serving the race by creating moral citizens. Therefore, it became apparent that by the time Few recommended an auditor for his school, the NRTIC president had become somewhat weary of hearing how many mistakes he had made. Moreover, Shepard's true search for advice in his correspondence with William Few was not on the operation of an institution, but on names of benefactors who would give to his institution. Nevertheless, Few understood that if Shepard's financial operation was lacking, donors would hesitate to give to his institution.[29]

Nevertheless, from 1915 to 1923, Shepard's school experienced a number of financial challenges that led to a series of name changes, with the state of North

Carolina ultimately taking control of the institution in 1923. The first name change occurred during the fall of 1915, when "the school was sold at public auction for the failure to pay back taxes to Thomas Gorman at $25,000." Notwithstanding such setbacks, Shepard did not give up on his dream of "changing the man" in North Carolina because he quickly reached out to those he called his northern financial "partners" to support his cause in regaining control of his institution. With the help of individuals such as B. N. Duke, Russell B. Sage, and Howard Chidley, Shepard was able to recover the school by October 31, 1915, under the name of the National Training School.[30]

After Shepard cleared one fiscal hurdle, another financial obstacle stood in his path. This time America's involvement in World War I was a chief contributor in the slowing of donations coming into the school in 1919 because of the residual impact of the war's end coupled with frayed race relations in the nation during the postwar period. According to North Carolina Central historians, from 1919 to 1923 the school virtually operated in the red, while perpetuating "its policy of open door[s] as it aided indigent students." With Shepard's primary focus going to the overall fiscal operation of the institution and the school's debt growing larger by the year, the board began to consider changing the environment in which the institution operated. While the school's objective of training ministers was a major selling point to both the black and white communities, the trustees grappled over the idea of whether one of the religious denominations should take control of the school. Importantly, there were already privately funded black colleges in North Carolina controlled by black churches during this era such as Johnson C. Smith College in Charlotte, North Carolina, which fell under the auspices of the Presbyterian Church and James Shepard's alma mater, Shaw University, located in Raleigh, North Carolina, which was affiliated with the Baptist Church. It is not clear why Shepard and his board of advisors decided against allowing one of the many denominations to take control of the fiscal operations of his institution, but one major issue that served as a deal breaker was the fact that the black church itself was a not-for-profit entity and therefore could have faced the same financial perils that Shepard's school was already experiencing.[31]

The second option eventually became the choice which Shepard and his trustees chose and that was to allow the state of North Carolina to gain control of his institution. That decision was also a risky one, as there were already state-supported black colleges in North Carolina, one of them being led by an advisor of Shepard's, James B. Dudley of the North Carolina A&M College in Greensboro, North Carolina. This risk was caused by Shepard's mission of "changing the man," by giving him morality which largely focused on a sound knowledge of liberal arts instruction. Therefore, if the state of North Carolina agreed to purchase the school and keep its mission, the National Training School would become the first state-supported liberal arts black college in North Carolina and arguably in the South. Dudley's school, on the other hand, focused on agricultural and mechanical training for African Americans, thus advancing the idea of a nonthreatening mission that appeased many conservative whites during the early twentieth century.[32]

Shepard's school made no such disclaimer as his mission was clearly stated in its original and second title. Nevertheless, in 1923 the state of North Carolina agreed to purchase the National Training School, changing its name to the Durham State Normal School. While it was no longer a private entity, neither the mission nor the leader of the school changed as the state's government officials agreed to keep James Shepard as the president of their new institution of higher education. This is significant as it reveals the respect that state officials had for Shepard in terms of developing a curriculum and employing appropriate faculty to help advance his race during the early twentieth century. With securing funds for the operations of the school off of Shepard's desk, he would have the ability to broaden the overall scope of the institution with the backing of the entire state of North Carolina. Importantly, Shepard was able to stay at the helm of his institution due to the partnerships he had created along the way. These individuals supported Shepard's desire to remain as the head of the newest state-supported black college in North Carolina.[33]

With a major burden for James Shepard being alleviated by the state of North Carolina, the years ahead of this administrator having to "walk the tightrope" became more difficult as individuals from both the white and black community began to demand the president's true positions on the issue of race relations. Notwithstanding these difficulties, the partnerships that Shepard created with philanthropists, educators, and clergy throughout the United States eventually placed him and his institution on a solid foundation. Therefore, the institution that became known as the North Carolina College for Negroes in 1925 became a major influence in the development of black life in the city of Durham and the state of North Carolina due to the groundwork that Shepard and his partners had laid during the formative years of the NRTIC.[34]

4

Behind Enemy Lines with No Beachhead

James E. Shepard's Relationship with the NAACP
during the Jim Crow Era

> But never forget that Durham is in the South and that around these 5,000 Negroes
> are twice as many whites who own most of the property, dominate the political
> life exclusively, and form the main current of social life. . . . As the editor of the
> local daily put it in a well deserved rebuke to former Governor Glenn of North
> Carolina: "If the Negro is going down, for God's sake let it be because of his own
> fault, and not because we are pushing him."
>
> *W. E. B. Du Bois*

As the bustling cold winter winds blew through the state capital of North
Carolina in January 1927, a warmly dressed James E. Shepard, president of the
North Carolina College for Negroes (NCC), formerly the National Religious
Training Institute and Chautauqua for the Negro Race (NRTIC), entered the
State Revenue building to conduct the business of his institution. Now in his
sixteenth year at the helm of a school that he founded, the forty-nine-year-
old black southerner waited patiently for a passenger elevator to carry him to
the appropriate floor while he was still warmly dressed in an overcoat and hat.
Rather than take the stairs, which would have surely avoided any racial misun-
derstandings, Shepard stood patiently awaiting the elevator's arrival. Once this
mechanical carriage appeared, Shepard allowed the white bystanders, some of
whom were state legislators, to board prior to his entrance. He understood the
social and racial etiquette of the South during this era. However, once on the
elevator, the NCC president failed to adhere to one custom that almost cost
his college state appropriations for the years of 1927 and 1928. Likely still trem-
bling from the gusty winter winds of North Carolina and also witnessing that
other male passengers failed to remove their hats in a crowded elevator, James

Shepard quietly took this journey to his proper floor without removing his hat while still in the presence of the white male legislators.[1]

Days later an angry O. B. Moss, state representative from Nash County, North Carolina, initiated a frontal assault on Shepard and NCC for the administrator's disrespect for the code of racial etiquette. Representative Moss, understanding the political support that James Shepard received from some state officials, proposed "to take the institution from under the supervision of the State Department of Public Instruction and put it in the hands of the board of directors." Such a move would have cost NCC some $200,000 in state appropriations. Moss justified his opposition by asserting, "As I rode up in the elevator the other day, I noticed its president rode up with his hat on although it was filled with white men." While this situation could have started a firestorm against the now mature administrator, partnerships in the state legislature that Shepard had built over the years proved beneficial. State representative Thomas J. Gold, a Democrat, came to Shepard's rescue, saying, "Don't you know there isn't room in those elevators in the Revenue building for a man to get his hand to his hat when there's a crowd of legislators." Sentiments of this sort likely led to Shepard's belief that he did not have to fully adhere to all of the racial and social norms of the day.[2]

Nevertheless, as cooler heads prevailed, Representative Reuben O. Everett of Durham recalled that "the relations between the Negroes and white people of Durham are most cordial and the white people there are able to command the respect of the Negro." Shortly thereafter, Shepard was informed of the discussions that had taken place in the state capital and "declared he had no recollections of having paid any slight to legislators" aboard the elevator.[3]

This oversight in observing the racial norms of the day served as the backdrop for the new battles that Shepard would face as president of NCC. The black college administrator entered an era when he could no longer "walk the tight rope" on the issue of race. Individuals from the white and black communities had demanded to know his true intentions on this issue. Therefore, this chapter will reveal Shepard's racial philosophy while he still served as the president of a now publicly funded black college in the segregated South. The argument of this chapter is that while James Shepard dealt with many complex racial situations during the Jim Crow Era in the Deep South, his ultimate goal was to uplift the race through his role as a black college president.[4]

To consider Shepard or any other black college president in the South during this era simply as a racial accommodationist for political decisions they publicly made is somewhat misleading. This type of classification adds to the false assumption that black southern leaders who were not radical in terms of race relations were self-serving, egotistical tyrants who only looked out for their own best interests. Therefore, to juxtapose these ideas, this chapter will argue that rather than being branded simply as an accommodationist, Shepard (and likely the vast majority of southern-based black college presidents during the Jim Crow Era) should be considered a pragmatist. This assessment is based on his desire to have not only his institution survive during an era before the civil rights movement but also to preserve his philosophy for racial uplift through the infusion of both classical and moral education, which in his mind were improving the conditions of his race in North Carolina.[5]

Months after the elevator incident, James Shepard began planning for the Durham Conference. He had the help of other prominent African Americans of Durham, who included two of his former business partners from the North Carolina Mutual and Provident Association (NCMPA), William G. Pearson and Charles C. Spaulding. The stated aim of this meeting was to discuss "matter[s] relating to financial, business, social, religious, educational, health, insurance, and political conditions of the race." Shepard had hosted a similar meeting in 1916, when he held an interracial conference on secondary and higher education at the NRTIC while still struggling to secure donors for his then-private institution. According to the *Norfolk Journal,* that particular meeting was attended by hundreds of participants and headlined by some of the most prominent "race leaders" of the day. Presenters included Joel Spingarn, the head of the National Association for the Advancement of Colored People (NAACP); W. E. B. Du Bois, intellectual and editor of that organization's magazine, *The Crisis*; and Kelly Miller, scholar and early advocate for Shepard's school.[6]

The interracial conference of 1916 successfully introduced ideas that advanced the African American community in Durham. In 1927 Shepard and his business colleagues wished to host another conference on race in their city to discuss the current issues that plagued southern black Americans. The idea of such a meeting likely came from Kelly Miller, who in 1925 argued that the race needed a "Negro Sanhedrin" that would discuss pertinent racial matters. Miller wanted this council to answer questions of racial prejudice and reveal to what extent this prejudice stifled the growth of the black community. Miller also argued that "the race as a whole had never hitherto seriously essayed [a] collective handling of the racial situation" and that therefore such a council needed to be assembled. While this call to action went out to black scholars across the nation, the creation of yet another race organization appeared unnecessary to some African Americans.[7]

This hesitation was likely due to the fact that Miller's call was aimed largely at bringing the black intellectual community together rather than discussing race relations with a more diverse group of African Americans. Some of Miller's critics, such as one *Pittsburgh Courier* editor, wrote that "the Negro Sanhedrin was launched with the best of intentions, but it had no clear-cut, challenging program" that would ultimately benefit the entire race. Such an argument reflected a broader rift between the black elite including intellectuals on the one hand, and the masses of the black community as a whole on the other, regarding the proper way to advance the race during the 1920s. Moreover, local leaders wanted a larger say about the role of their communities in the racial uplift of their area rather than simply waiting for "outsiders" to dictate their agenda.[8]

The Durham Conference was centered on community building. The ideals of community building were central to such institutions as the NCMPA and NCC. According to historian Walter Weare, the NCMPA and NCC in the city of Durham were sources of inspiration for the local African American community. They "provided the distinctive features of black Durham and kept it from being seen as a dreary, slum-filled industrial settlement of migrant tobacco workers." Both institutions created a class of prominent, black middle-class leaders who could possibly help solve the race problem in North Carolina. Therefore, the Durham Conference had legitimacy because it was spearheaded by Pearson, Spaulding, and Shepard, the creators and guardians of Durham's black middle class.[9]

Fusing the concerns of local leaders and the ideas of black intellectuals, the Durham Conference was called to convene on December 7, 1927. Although some appreciated the idea of this conference being scheduled in a southern city, the organizers dealt with criticisms from the black press. The press was mainly critical on the point that meetings of this sort were "wasting a great deal of time by the way in diversions fruitful only in accumulating disillusionment and hopelessness." Therefore, when the time came to recruit national black leaders and intellectuals to attend this meeting, some appeared reluctant.[10]

Shepard, as secretary of the Durham Conference and president of the NCC, reached out early to W. E. B. Du Bois. On August 22, 1927, Shepard informed Du Bois of the plans for having a conference in Durham that would discuss issues facing the race. Desiring to have a fruitful meeting that would actually produce results, Shepard hoped Du Bois could come to Durham prior to the conference to "outline a program so that no mistakes will be made and some tangible results accomplished." The Durham Conference committee wanted substantial results to come from this meeting as they clearly understood that many had a critical image of local and national leaders as being mere pontificators.[11]

Du Bois initially appeared hesitant to lend his support to this cause. Echoing similar sentiments of some of the press, the scholar informed Shepard that he hated to see "the number of Negro organizations multiply." Du Bois nevertheless lent his support and planned to travel to North Carolina in September 1927 to help the committee members prepare for their December meeting.[12]

The Durham Conference began to take shape and a clear agenda was set in place at the committee's September meeting. The new title for their December meeting was the "Stock-Taking and Fact Finding Conference on the American Negro." The attendees could expect to hear paper presentations on topics such as work and wage; retail business, commerce, and manufacturing; savings credit and insurance; religious beliefs and activities; political situations; elementary, high school, and college education; health and home life; and crime and social uplift. Each of these subjects would be discussed by an "expert in the field," with Du Bois leading the conversation on black politics. Shepard asked the scholar to "present a paper on the subject, also a documentary [primary source evidence, such as surveys] on [the] present conditions" of black suffrage in the United States.[13]

Yet Du Bois had a slightly different vision. "What the conference ought to present before it," he believed, "would be a compilation of the best facts obtainable so that they would be in a position [to] judge exactly present conditions [of black suffrage in America]." Du Bois forwarded Shepard an article that he planned to publish in *The Crisis* in November 1927 that revealed statistics of African American voting and the condition of race relations in several states. The scholar further explained that this type of report should be conducted in Durham, which would reveal the true race relations of that city and state.[14]

With intellectuals such as Du Bois on board to present at this conference, the focus shifted to the local leaders. The Stock-Taking Conference sought to incorporate the everyday lives of the citizens of Durham. To do this, conference organizers highlighted one of NCC's programs. On September 28, 1927, Shepard announced that his college would create a school of business administration. This new program at NCC fit into the first four aims of the Stock-Taking Conference. Moreover, such a program would prepare the next generation of black entrepreneurs, insurance agents, bankers, and retailers, solidifying the black middle class of Durham for generations to come.[15]

Besides this academic program, Shepard considered the greater difficulties facing African Americans. Ten days after the conference commenced, Shepard and other presenters used the findings of the meeting to speak out against the horrors of racial lynchings in the South. For example, Shepard issued a call for a day of prayer to "Wipe out Lynching" on February 12, 1928. Using data from the Stock-Taking Conference, he argued that by November 1927, more than four thousand people had been lynched in the American South. Accordingly, Shepard argued that this type of injustice "leaves a stain on all of us," referring to citizens of all races of the United States.[16]

Finally, Shepard issued a charge for a serious conversation that would take place in black churches across the country. He encouraged black ministers to craft their sermons around several issues that plagued the black community. Importantly, Shepard gave these ministers a list of topics to discuss for the upcoming year, which included:

"What is the Ideal Christian Brotherhood in Race Relations?" "The Opportunity of the Christian Church for Promoting Better Race Relations in America," "The Challenge of the Race Question to Christian Missions and American Democracy," "Fundamental Feelings and Attitudes Between Races," "American Indian Life and History," "The Lynching Evil and its Effects Upon American Life," "Contributions of Negroes to American Music and Literature," "Present Provision to Negro Education," "Migration of the Negro to the Cities and its Effects," "The Significance of the Negro Church in American Life," "Mutual Interest of the White and Negro in Race and Health, Housing and Industry," and "Contacts with Orientals."[17]

While Shepard and the members of the Stock-Taking Conference were releasing their agendas for the black community for the upcoming year, the NAACP continued its fight against racial injustices throughout the nation. Importantly, the NAACP had had a presence in the Tar Heel State since 1917. During that year, three chapters of this civil rights organization were established in Raleigh, Greensboro, and Durham. Although initially small in membership, the NAACP gained most recruits as a consequence of violence perpetrated against African Americans. According to its acting secretary, James Weldon Johnson, "There is no doubt that a new spirit is awakening in the South and that the National Association for the Advancement of Colored People offers the precise medium for the exercise of that spirit." Shortly thereafter, NAACP branches sprang up throughout the state with local branches existing in every major North Carolina city by 1920. Consequently, by that year there were approximately 1,075 members in North Carolina's NAACP.[18]

The emergence of the NAACP in North Carolina by 1917 was sparked by a number of factors, none larger than the race riots that occurred in East St. Louis, Missouri, and Houston, Texas. In February 1917, the Aluminum Ore Company in East St. Louis hired 470 black workers to replace white members of the American Federation of Labor (AFL) who were striking. Angered by the hiring of these strikebreakers coupled with the fear of permanent job loss, several white AFL members wanted to retaliate against these black workers. On July 1, the white strikers drove through the black neighborhood of East St. Louis firing shots. After the AFL rioters left, two white plainclothes police offers drove into the same neighborhood and were shot and killed by black residents who likely believed the drive-by shooters had returned. Shortly thereafter, an angry white mob returned to the black community for revenge. During its acts of vengeance, African Americans were mutilated and killed, and their lifeless bodies were tossed into the Mississippi River. Joining in this massacre were white police officers, who eventually helped burn and destroy hundreds of homes in this black community. By the time this violence ended, thirty-five blacks and eight whites had been murdered.[19]

One month later, similar violence ensued in Houston, Texas. This race riot occurred on August 23, 1917, when a black soldier from the Third Battalion of the Twenty-Fourth Infantry tried to prevent a white police officer, Lee Sparks, from assaulting a black woman. Angered by this act, Sparks clubbed the soldier and carried him to jail. While investigating this case, Corporal Charles W. Baltimore was also beaten and incarcerated. A few hours later, both soldiers were released. Nevertheless, rumors circulated that Baltimore had been murdered, which led black soldiers to seek revenge. Sergeant Vida Henry rallied more than one hundred black soldiers in a two-hour assault on the police station. Fifteen white residents—including five police officers—one Mexican American, four black soldiers, and two black civilians were killed. After the riot ceased, the US Army arrested 118 black soldiers, 63 of whom were charged with mutiny. After their court martialing, Corporal Baltimore and twelve other soldiers were hanged. Later seven others were executed, while another seven were acquitted and the remainder were sentenced to prison from two years to the remainder of their lives. Notwithstanding his role in this riot, Sparks was allowed to return to his post as a police officer where he later killed two black people that same year.[20]

These two race riots became the catalyst for African Americans' desire to fight for their human rights. In both cases, when the blacks displayed a willingness to either protect themselves or retaliate against mob violence, the scales of justice always weighed against them. Rather than give in to these circumstances, however, organizations such as the NAACP capitalized on them by expanding their memberships and creating a stronger alliance with liberal, white Republicans for protecting African Americans' civil liberties. Not only did this violence spark a grassroots movement within the black community; it also provided the Republican Party an opportunity to pass legislation that would provide protection for its base.[21]

With the NAACP gaining traction in North Carolina and other southern states, two Republican congressmen, Leonidas C. Dyer of St. Louis and Merrill Moores of Indianapolis, introduced a federal antilynching bill, which was enthusiastically endorsed by the civil rights organization. Dyer sought to have this bill passed after the horrific race riots of East St. Louis and Houston. If passed, this new legislation would make acts of terrorism such as lynching federal crimes. Along with the desire to have this bill passed, Dyer, Moores, and their fellow Republican supporters wanted to gain control of Congress and the White House. Therefore, the fall elections of 1920 would serve as yet another opportunity for the black community (at least those who were not disenfranchised) to vote for a group of individuals who would help end injustices that were taking place against them.[22]

With the support of the NAACP and northern black voters, the fall elections of 1920 saw large Republican victories in the congressional and presidential elections. This gave the Republican Party a unique opportunity to pass the Dyer Bill. While campaigning, Warren G. Harding publicly proclaimed that he, along with the Republican Party, would look for the most effective ways to end lynching. Shortly after he was elected, President Harding argued in a special message to Congress that it "ought to wipe the stain of barbaric lynching from the banners of a free and orderly representative democracy."[23]

By the fall of 1921, debate on the antilynching bill had reached Congress. African Americans around the nation likely felt that the federal government would finally pass a law that would effectively uphold the Fourteenth Amendment. Nonetheless, the deliberations on this bill were very heated as the ostensibly true issue came down to states' rights, which was actually a cover for the race issue. For example, southern Democrats argued that the passage of such a bill would give the federal government too much authority over the states and local judicial systems. Northern Republicans countered that argument by citing the lack of justice for black defendants in southern courts and jails. According to Republican congressmen, if the South protected all of its citizens under the Fourteenth Amendment, the issue of the Dyer legislation would be a moot point. Notwithstanding the early back and forth, the bill was finally brought to a vote at the end of January 1922, easily winning passage in the House of Representatives by 230 to 119 votes.[24]

Sadly, the victory represented by the passage of this bill in the House was short-lived. James Weldon Johnson knew that passage in the Senate would be a much tougher battle. Throughout the spring and summer of 1923, Johnson and the NAACP campaigned to keep this bill at the forefront of the American landscape. Due to the NAACP's grassroots organizing ability and the fact that the Republicans controlled Congress, the Dyer Bill was scheduled for debate in fall of 1923. Understanding that they did not have the votes to defeat this bill, southern Democrats used the filibuster to delay the congressional vote.[25]

The manner in which the Democrats filibustered this bill was new. During this filibuster, Democrats had no desire to prolong the time of the debate so that they might gain an understanding of the bill or to have Democratic amendments placed in the measure Their true desire was to have the bill removed from the schedule altogether. After hours of this filibuster, Republicans finally caved in and allowed the Dyer Anti-Lynching Bill's removal from the debate schedule. Johnson and members of the NAACP quickly reached out to Republican congressmen and President Harding to gain future support for this bill to no avail. According to historian Patricia Sullivan, the lack of fight in the Republican Party caused African Americans to shift from solid Republican to political independence. Consequently, the effort to pass antilynching legislation would be the fight of the 1920s for the NAACP and other pro–civil rights groups throughout the nation.[26]

After the Dyer Bill failed, the NAACP and other black organizations continued to push for legislative support for the passage of antilynching legislation. Such organizations as the Grand Lodge of North Carolina Masons and Order of Eastern Stars donated two hundred dollars to the NAACP to support this cause in 1928. Also, the participants in the Stock-Taking Conference issued a public appeal for the end of lynching by calling for a day of prayer to "whip out the evils of lynchings." Importantly for this study, James E. Shepard was very active in both the Grand Lodge and the Order of Eastern Stars during the 1920s.[27]

With the NAACP's chief focus during the 1920s centered on eradicating lynchings, Shepard still believed that the way to advance the black community was through the church and its leaders. From Shepard's perspective, the church could best highlight black contributions to the arts and the economy as well as travesties such as lynchings. He also wanted more African American involvement in the political process, so that publicly funded black colleges could eventually receive their fair share of state assistance. Therefore, Shepard was placing the onus on the black clergy to spread the message of facts from the Stock-Taking Conference to the masses of the black community.[28]

Consequently, the leaders of the Stock-Taking Conference elected Dr. Shepard as the chairman of the conference for the upcoming year. Shepard did not take his role as chairman lightly. Nor did media outlets hold back any punches in their queries concerning the true purpose of the Durham Conference. Within weeks of his election as the chairman of the conference, Shepard was inundated with requests from the black press pertaining to the findings of the Stock-Taking Conference and the role that this new organization would have in uplifting the race. The new chairman issued a press release asking the black media for time for the authors and presenters of the conference to fully compile their information for publication. Shepard wanted to make sure that once the findings of the conference were released, "mere opinion [would] be omitted" from the published record. He hoped this document would provide "authentic facts regarding the Negro in America which, for their wide range, care of collection and authenticity, will hardly be equaled by anything at present available in print."[29]

Shepard's status as a race leader increased in the late 1920s. For example, in February 1928, the NCC president endorsed the ideals of the Harlem Renaissance by encouraging young black children to enter their artistic works for the opportunity to win a prize that he sponsored. According to Shepard and journalist George S. Schuyler, the director of the judging committee, "the awards [and paintings were] designed to stimulate the artistic bent of Negro children." Shepard's choice of Schuyler to serve as head of this committee illustrates the role the NCC's president felt the Harlem Renaissance should play in America. This answer was made clear by Schuyler two years earlier when he penned an article titled "The Negro-Art Hokum," which appeared in *The Nation* in June 1926. In that piece, the journalist asserted that the "concept of 'Negro art' was bogus" and from his perspective was "self-evident foolishness."[30]

Schuyler likely wrote this article in response to Alain Locke's call for black artists to incorporate African art with modern works. Locke believed that not only would infusing African art with "modern" art reveal African heritage to blacks, it would also debunk negative images that were being portrayed of blacks in modern art. Schuyler, on the other hand, believed that black artists should not be confined to simply incorporating African art with modern art. The journalist argued that black artists were as diverse as white artists and should not be confined to simply depicting the positive aspects of African art. Consequently, Schuyler proclaimed that "the literature, painting, and sculpture of Aframericans—such as there is—is identical in kind with the literature, painting, and sculpture of white Americans: that is, it shows more or less evidence of European influence." Simply put, according to Schuyler, by merging African art with modern art, "the Aframerican is merely a lamp blacked Anglo-Saxon."[31]

Although their theories for the Harlem Renaissance were more conservative than those of Alain Locke and other pioneers of this artistic movement, Shepard and Schuyler received entries for their competition from young African Americans from cities all over the country. These cities included Troy, North Carolina; Vinita, Oklahoma; St. Louis, Missouri; Birmingham, Alabama; Port Arthur, Texas; New York City, New York; Shinnston, West Virginia; Marshall, Texas; Tallahassee, Florida; Rock Castle, Virginia; Downingtown, Pennsylvania; and Coatesville, Pennsylvania. Members of the black middle class from across the nation likely appreciated Shepard's emphasis on understanding and appreciating African American culture through art. Also, such a program reveals that NCC's president was currently well aware of the issues confronting the black community nationwide.[32]

Later in the spring of 1928, Shepard cemented his role as the spokesman for his race in the city of Durham. The Duke University president, Dr. William Preston Few, had just begun a seminar series on southern race relations. Shepard had always had good relations with the presidents of Trinity College/Duke University. On several occasions, he invited the former president, John C. Kilgo, to speak before his student body, and he later asked Dr. Few for support in gaining benefactors for his then-private institution. The admiration appeared mutual. In March 1928, Few extended an invitation to Shepard to have a frank conversation with his white student body about race relations.[33]

The NCC president could have easily turned down this offer with the understanding that no matter what he said would be met with strong opposition from either side. However, the chairman of the Durham Conference answered the call and spoke to the white student body of Duke University on this highly sensitive subject. Shepard began his address by informing the audience of the difficulties that white people had in understanding "the position of the Negro" in the American South. He gave a specific example of a current misconception of the American Negro. "The Negro will steal," the president initially proclaimed in gaining the attention of the audience. The idea "has been repeated so often that it is the commonly accepted measure of the morals of the race."[34]

Dr. Shepard then evoked a high profile case of bribery and theft that involved

President Warren G. Harding's administration and an oil company based in Wyoming in 1924. "Yet, a gigantic steal like the Teapot Dome may take place in which more is stolen than a similar group of Negroes could ever steal in a lifetime, without stigmatizing the white race as a race of thieves." Many listeners had likely never heard a southern African American leader criticize a white authority figure for acts of corruption. Moreover, he juxtaposed this corruption to comparatively petty acts of black crime. The NCC president thus encouraged the students, faculty, staff, and administration of Duke University not to group all African Americans together in terms of negative stereotypes, especially since there were negative elements in the white community that did not serve as the marker of their entire race.[35]

Shepard now moved to the heart of his address, which centered on equal justice and the black community's right to vote for elected officials. Juries were "almost invariably made up of whites and that thus, rarely did the Negro at the bar of justice have a chance for a fair and impartial trial." Therefore, Shepard argued that more blacks should be chosen to serve as jurors so that when African Americans faced the judge and jury, they would in turn be judged by a jury of their peers.[36]

"Speaking from the fullness of his heart," Shepard relayed that many black Durhamites wanted him to send the message that the African American community deserved the vote. "The right to vote was essential to the Negro's welfare," he proclaimed. Moreover, Shepard cautioned his audience that the act of voting would not merely lead blacks to the false ecstasy of celebrating their "political spoils." Rather, through the vote, the black community would be in a position to help itself. If given the opportunity to vote, Shepard proclaimed, blacks "might share more equitably in civic improvements such as better streets, paving, sewerage, etc." Shepard spoke to the basic needs in the black community and the importance of officials that were duly elected by the black community.[37]

Despite his pleas for the black vote and his condemnation of President Harding's role in the Tea Pot Dome scandal during his lecture at Duke, Shepard's status grew in North Carolina. Consequently, NCC began to reap the dividends of his work. In September 1928, the state of North Carolina appropriated $150,000 to expand the administration building on the campus of NCC. According to news reports, the North Carolina legislature in the upcoming years was expected to "make liberal provisions for maintenance and improvement purposes and enable the officers to forge rapidly ahead in their efforts to make the institution the leading college in this section" of the country. NCC was embarking on yet another milestone; in June 1929, its first graduating class would complete a course of study. Therefore, the college would have reached "its full stature as a Grade A senior college, devoted exclusively to the training of young men and women." James E. Shepard was clearly emerging as a significant force in the state of North Carolina and the South as a whole.[38]

With the changing political and social climate, Shepard was no longer shielded from personal and political attacks. His vision for the black community began to be challenged by other race leaders, including Kelly Miller, an early advocate of Shepard's school. When the Durham committee issued the announcement for the second annual Stock-Taking Conference, Miller responded with sharp criticism. In his opinion, "mere ascertainment of detailed facts about politics, economics, education and industry is but tickling the surface without affecting the fundamental facts of race prejudice, of which politics, education and economic proscription are but indications." Miller thought that like his own Negro Sanhedrin, the Stock-Taking Conference was missing the goal of truly solving the race problem in America. The scholar proposed that leaders should "develop or devise a sustaining philosophy to guide our way amidst the difficulties and vicissitudes which so easily beset us." Miller closed his attack on the Stock-Taking Conference as follows: "The ax must be laid at the foot of the tree. It is but a waste of while to spend much further time in pruning away decadent limbs which spring from internal disease."[39]

Notwithstanding this criticism, Shepard and the Durham Conference forged ahead in the spring of 1929. Among the 250 leaders who were present at the conference was Kelly Miller. Shepard and his committee made clear their efforts to attract broad segments of the black community. In a press release, the group stated that "all discussion will be open, free and frank and the hope is expressed that some definite conclusions and plans can be reached for carrying out the facts ascertained at the conference." The Durham Conference committee not only wanted to put these black leaders at ease, but also to speak to the masses of the black community.[40]

According to the official press release, "careful consideration and attention will be given to all matters of interest to the Negro." Discussions would take place on hospital availability in the black community, business and its role in promoting the black community, literature and its role in shaping the current cultural experience, the number of African Americans who actually voted in the elections of 1928, and how public school funds were divided. This agenda is a clear indicator that the conference was evolving as there was no item discussing black-white race relations. Rather, the conversation centered on the idea of black self-help.[41]

As the second annual Durham Conference commenced on April 17, 1929, the committee made a conscious effort to have every group in the African American community represented by making a presentation. For example, discussing the role of African American women was Miss Nannie H. Burroughs of Washington, DC, while two prominent educational leaders, John Hope, president of Morehouse College, and Mordecai Johnson, president of Howard University, talked about the role of black colleges. An array of clergy, businessmen, and educators at the second annual conference represented a number of states in the union. The attendees did not merely come to Durham to enjoy the local cuisine or the church services that would be rendered at the White Rock Baptist Church; they came to set the agenda for the black community for the upcoming year.[42]

The attendees ended their conference with a resolution to spark some sort of agency in their communities. Echoing similar ideas from Shepard's presentation at Duke University in the spring of 1928, the fact finders issued a resolution to President Herbert Hoover that called for more African American involvement in law enforcement. "The conference recommended and respectfully requested President Hoover to appoint a Negro on the Law Enforcement Commission," the resolution read. The president had previously expressed a desire to create a Law Enforcement Commission that would investigate corruption in law enforcement agencies around the country. Therefore, Chairman Shepard was authorized by the conference to forward the resolution to the president, while also making a strong appeal for an African American to serve on this new commission. "The Negro has been the greatest sufferer from failures to enforce the law," the fact finders informed President Hoover, and from their perspective blacks were the group that had experienced the greatest violations of human rights.[43]

This resolution was clearly an attempt of the fact finders to address the issue of lynchings. From their standpoint, if an African American served on the law enforcement commission, that individual would have the ability to hold local law enforcement agencies accountable. Although Shepard and the fact finders were not overtly demanding antilynching legislation, they were asking for the federal government to enforce the current laws and to hold local and state governments accountable for not upholding the laws. In essence, they were asking for the same thing that was previously proposed in the Dyer Bill.[44]

At the conclusion of another successful Stock-Taking Conference, Shepard and the NCC began to reap the benefits of hosting this meeting on racial uplift. Not only did he gain exposure by hosting this event on the campus, but he also bolstered his institution's image in the minds of African American leaders. With this rise in national prominence came a greater appreciation from state and local officials in North Carolina. This rise likely came because his message of racial uplift was not as forceful as that of that of Walter White and the NAACP. Therefore, in July 1929 the state announced plans to appropriate more than $100,000 for the building of a women's dormitory on the campus of NCC, which would eventually house more than one hundred female students. Shepard's school finally received the local, state, and national recognition that he felt it deserved. This acknowledgement was largely due to the role that he played in the Durham Conference and likely the interactions that his faculty, staff, and students had with key members of the black community there. As Shepard rose in relevance on the national stage, white legislators in North Carolina appreciated the growth of NCC. Ironically, this approval came after his powerful address at Duke and only two years after he overlooked the southern code of racial etiquette, which almost cost his school state appropriations altogether. In the late 1920s and early 1930s, Shepard and NCC cemented their legacies for generations to come.[45]

While Shepard's star continued to rise in North Carolina, the NAACP was making plans for a final push at gaining legislative support to make lynching a federal crime. Also, this group entered this phase of its fight against mob violence with Walter White serving as its new leader. This change was due to the retirement of James Weldon Johnson from the NAACP to become the first Adam K. Spence Professor of Creative Literature at Fisk University. Although Johnson's legacy as secretary of the NAACP was solidified in the 1920s by the growth in the number of branches and members throughout the nation, his retirement coincided with the Scottsboro Case and a rise of African American involvement with the Communist Party.[46]

The watershed moment that made the Communist Party a viable group for southern blacks occurred in the early spring of 1931. On March 25 of that year, nine young black men jumped on a freight train traveling west through northern Alabama. Once the black youths were aboard the train, they were approached by a group of white men and two white women. Shortly thereafter, a fight broke out among the men that lasted until the train was stopped in Paint Rock, Alabama. Once in Paint Rock, a mob of white men seized the nine black youths and quickly accused them of raping the two white women. Consequently, the black men were taken to Scottsboro, Alabama, where they narrowly escaped a local lynch mob.[47]

Without finances to secure proper legal assistance, the nine black men were tried by all-white juries within days of arriving in Scottsboro. Eight of the nine were convicted of raping the two women and sentenced to death, which delighted some white southerners. Initially unsure of the innocence of the young men accused of raping two white women, the NAACP appeared hesitant to lend support for the nine young men and their families in this case. While the leaders of this organization debated whether or not to support the Scottsboro nine, or Scottsboro Boys as they came to be known, the Communist-affiliated International Labor Defense (ILD) took over the appeals process for the young men. After years of appeals, the last of the nine men were finally freed in 1950 as it was proven that none of them had raped the two women.[48]

The Scottsboro case served only as one of the catalysts for southern African American support for the Communist Party. The party's philosophy regarding class and racial identity was also appealing. Although Johnson and White did not disagree with the Communist Party's agenda of covering workers' rights, civil rights, and pan-African solidarity, they did feel that this agenda was too broad. Moreover, with J. Edgar Hoover and the Federal Bureau of Investigation (FBI) labeling black civil rights organizations as communist plots to destroy the United States of America, the NAACP wanted to separate themselves from a connection with such a stigma.[49]

Not only did 1931 mark the end of an era for the NAACP with the retirement of James Weldon Johnson and a leaking of support from some poor black southerners, it was also a tragic year for the new secretary, Walter White. On November 16, 1931, George White, Walter White's father—a graduate of Atlanta University who was a postal worker in Atlanta, Georgia, which helped place his family in the black middle class in Atlanta during the late nineteenth and early twentieth centuries—was hit by an automobile while walking home from his daughter Madeline's home in Atlanta, Georgia. After George left her home, he was expected to call Madeline once he arrived back at his residence. When this call failed to arrive, she left in search of her father and found him in poor condition on the corner of Houston and Piedmont. Witnessing the condition that he was in, Madeline ran to retrieve their family physician, only to return to find her father missing. According to Walter White's biographer, Kenneth Janken, because of George White's light complexion, someone likely found him and assumed that he was an elderly white man who had been involved in an accident. When she could not locate her father, Madeline went to the black ward of Grady Hospital in search of him. After conducting a thorough search of the black ward's records, she realized that he was not there. Then she went across the street to the white ward where she found her father receiving "good care." Shortly thereafter, George was transferred to the black ward once the doctors found out that he was a "Negro."[50]

Five days after he heard of his father's accident and that he was slipping in and out of consciousness, Walter White traveled to Atlanta to see his father presumably before he died. After two weeks, the seventy-four-year-old died due to complications from the accident. Although this passing of his father was tragic for Walter and his family, he used the events surrounding the death of George White to fight against the system of segregation.[51]

Ironically, the story that Walter told *Harper's Weekly* was more sensational than the one Madeline told him. Arguing that he was still angry about the death of his father, White recalled that the Jim Crow customs in the South were largely responsible for the passing of his father. Desiring to explain the incident, White recalled that after the white attendants recognized that George was black, one shouted in disgust, "What! Have we got a nigger over here on the white side?" Then, after his father was "gingerly but speedily" transferred to the black ward, White said that the segregated conditions of the black ward led to the demise of his father because of the lack of equipment and expertise in treating a patient with such traumatic wounds.[52]

When asked by his sister why he told such a fabricated tale about the mistreatment of their father at Grady Hospital, White informed her that he desired to capture the attention of the white press and reveal the discrepancies of care that African Americans received in black facilities as opposed to white facilities. Consequently, White felt that his story was not necessarily about his father per se, but the story of southern black fathers who actually endured the same segregation-related mistreatment that White embellished in his tale. Therefore, he used the death of his father as a prime example of how the idea of separate but equal was a fallacy by explaining that even members of the black social elite did not receive proper care under segregated customs. Importantly, White used this story to pivot the NAACP's attention from mob violence to fighting more aggressively against segregation.[53]

Meanwhile, the struggle for racial advancement in North Carolina began to shift quickly beneath James Shepard's feet. A segment of the black community began seeking more radical means of black progress rather than the gradual approach to which Shepard and other black leaders were accustomed. NCC's president was not the only black leader attacked for taking a staunchly gradual approach to racial uplift; Charles C. Spaulding and William G. Pearson shared in receiving such criticism from their younger counterparts. But for Shepard, this new strategy for racial uplift would possibly serve as an attack on the very existence of his institution.[54]

After a series of defeats pertaining to antilynching legislation, Walter White and the NAACP began to attack Republicans who refused to support such statutes. White started to openly challenge Republican president Herbert Hoover, first by not supporting his candidates for federal positions, including John J. Parker, Hoover's nominee for the US Supreme Court, and finally by endorsing a Democrat for the presidency of the United States in 1932. Shortly thereafter, White's attention shifted from securing an antilynching bill to ending segregation, which would prove as difficult a task.[55]

This choice was more taxing for southern black leaders as the association was no longer merely attacking "terrorism," but rather the southern way of life in general. Simply, White and the NAACP by 1930 had begun to fight for the desegregation of higher education in the South. While gradualist black leaders such as James Shepard had previously been staunch supporters of the NAACP, he now found himself in the precarious situation of having to defend his institution against claims levied by this civil rights organization. Shepard and other black college presidents were forced to choose to either fight for the survival of their institutions or for the causes of the NAACP during the 1930s and 1940s. Sadly, this era marked a time when many black college administrators received the label of accommodationist because they chose to openly fight for their schools rather than openly support the NAACP.[56]

James E. Shepard was likely the first black college administrator to actually face this choice when he was forced to act in the Thomas Hocutt case in 1933. In the early 1930s, members of the NAACP in Durham began to devise a plan that would attack the Jim Crow laws in higher education. No black college in North Carolina in the 1930s had law or pharmacy programs, so the local NAACP challenged the Jim Crow laws in higher education. This cause was spearheaded by William G. Pearson's nephew, Conrad O. Pearson, and his colleague, Cecil McCoy. They wanted to help one of James E. Shepard's students, Thomas Hocutt, integrate the University of North Carolina pharmacy school. For Shepard, the timing of this episode could not have been worse, as by 1933 the Great Depression was crippling the state's budget. Shepard had struggled to secure funds for his institution when it was private, and he also realized that the final authority over NCC rested with the governor and the state legislators. Therefore, he understood that he was in a situation which he must handle with extreme caution.[57]

While the NAACP was gearing up for a fight in state courts, Shepard and the other "old guards" of black Durham met to discuss their actions in considering the integration of the UNC pharmacy school. NCC's president also met with the southern white liberal Frank Porter Graham, who was also the president of UNC. Shepard came to the conclusion that the best action in this matter was to block Hocutt's transcript from being released to the UNC registrar. Not clearly understanding the resistance of some leaders in the black community but knowing the challenge that they would face from southern whites, the NAACP dispatched William Hastie, a former Howard University law professor, to litigate this case. While Hastie appeared well prepared for these proceedings and intending to fight for Hocutt's entrance into UNC's pharmacy program based on the principles of the United States Constitution, he and the NAACP failed to cover one minor detail: Hocutt's full eligibility to gain admittance into UNC. When UNC registrar Thomas Wilson was asked why Hocutt was denied admittance, the answer likely surprised those who attended the case. The registrar responded that Hocutt did not fully complete his application by submitting an official transcript with his package. The Thomas Hocutt case was subsequently defeated because James Shepard had refused to release the transcripts of his student.[58]

Prior to the case being settled, Pearson wrote White a note informing the NAACP's secretary of the proceedings. Hocutt's local attorney informed White that the North Carolina attorney general's office had encouraged Hocutt and his legal team not to sue; in return the office guaranteed that "certain officials would see that something was done towards educating the Negro in professional schools." In response to that request, Hastie countered that they would accept that deal "if the judgment would recite the names of these officials that would sponsor the movement." Not desiring to reveal its sources, the attorney general's staff rejected that request and then suggested again that they accept the avoidance of a suit when Hocutt and Hastie countered by asking for a continuance, by which Hastie was attempting to keep the case open despite the legal challenges he was facing by the state. Judge M. V. Barnhill denied the continuance, citing "Hocutt's failure to satisfy the requirements of 'necessary evidence of scholastic qualifications.'"[59]

Shortly after this case, Shepard came under attack from the NAACP and other "radicals." Walter White became a staunch opponent of Shepard and his fellow gradualist leaders of black Durham. It is clear, however, that like the vast majority of southern black leaders who actually had institutions to run, there was no beachhead to shield them from the backlash of the Jim Crow Era if they chose to join the radicals in backing swift action. In return for his gradualism, Shepard's school was later awarded with graduate programs. These programs kept the races segregated in higher education but also continued to produce qualified black citizens who would be equipped to tackle the vicissitudes of their era.[60]

Had Shepard joined the NAACP in this matter, his school would most likely not have received the appropriations for graduate programs and would have probably lost funds needed to exist altogether. Shepard, Spaulding, and Pearson operated in the lion's den of the Jim Crow South, while White and his NAACP colleagues fought against racial discrimination within the protection of northern state borders. Yet Shepard's decision to withhold Hocutt's transcript appears parochial. Shepard was not in line with the NAACP's aggressive approach for the national, long-term struggle to end segregation; he was focused on the local, long-term struggle to alleviate racial injustice by providing black North Carolinians an adequate education at NCC. Importantly, unlike the NAACP, Shepard and other black college presidents felt that their colleges were well suited to educate the black community during this era. Their aspiration during the pre–civil rights movement years was not to desegregate higher education but to have state and federal governments fund their institutions more equitably. This point is best highlighted by an answer that Shepard gave to the UNC Alumni Association. When asked by this group how he felt about NCC becoming affiliated with or seized by UNC, Shepard informed the group that he was strongly against the idea, saying "I believe Negroes should control their own colleges so as to develop self-consciousness and racial leadership."[61]

After 1933 many of Shepard's accomplishments as the chairman of the Stock-Taking Conference and president of NCC became overshadowed by his decision to withhold Thomas Hocutt's transcripts for admittance into UNC's pharmacy program. Moreover, black and white radicals alike began to define his legacy by arguing that Shepard accommodated white supremacists in order to "keep higher education segregated." The role that Shepard played in Durham's racial uplift becomes somewhat obfuscated by labeling him as an accommodationist. It fails to acknowledge the role that NCC played in the black community of Durham. It also fails to examine the changing philosophies of the NAACP and how these changes affected southern black leaders. Not only were these local southern black leaders placed in a compromising position by the agenda set by a national group, but the institutions in which they operated were placed in jeopardy due to the NAACP's new approach for civil rights. While Shepard made some accommodationist choices to benefit his institution, this institution helped build the black middle class in North Carolina.[62]

5

Are You For Me or Against Me?

The Political Life of James E. Shepard

The story of North Carolina's politics is nuanced,
multilayered, and at times contradictory.

Rob Christensen, The Paradox of Tar Heel Politics

After the presidential election of 1932, politics for the African American community were no longer politics as usual. After earning their right to vote with
the passage of the Fifteenth Amendment, African Americans became staunch
supporters of the Republican Party. From 1870 until the early 1930s, the Party
of Lincoln could count on the votes of the vast majority of the African American community (or at least of those individuals who were not disenfranchised).
While the black community voted for this party as a bloc for more than two
generations, their support was not rewarded with racially progressive legislation. With the Great Depression of the early 1930s and the rise of unprosecuted
race-based hate crimes such as lynchings, a segment of the black community
decided to sever its ties with the Party of Lincoln and join the political party
that once was a proud proponent of all-white primaries. A new day had come for
the Democratic Party, and it was ushered in by Franklin and Eleanor Roosevelt
with the help of some disillusioned black voters like Walter White, the secretary
of the NAACP, and Mary McLeod Bethune, the founding president of the private Bethune-Cookman College and advisor to Eleanor Roosevelt, who were in
search of a political party that would give them more than the meager results
that the Republicans had granted for generations.[1]

It is important to note, however, that the final shift from the Republican
Party to the Democratic Party did not occur until 1964, when a majority of
the African American community rewarded Democratic presidential candidate
Lyndon B. Johnson for his leadership in enacting the Civil Rights Act of that

year. This vote for Johnson can also be viewed as a vote against the Republican candidate Barry Goldwater and the Republican Party because not only did Goldwater vote against civil rights legislation, but he also considered civil rights demonstrations "crime in the streets." One hundred years after African Americans were freed from the horrors of slavery, a paradigm shift occurred: a majority of the black electorate cast its ballots for the Democratic Party (the party that "gave" them civil rights). This paradigm shift in black politics occurred because of the lack of legislative support that African Americans received from the GOP during the 1930s.[2]

For prominent black Republicans such as James E. Shepard, president of NCC, the 1930s also ushered in an era of more radical opposition against his gradual stance on civil rights. Particularly, Shepard's decision to withhold Thomas Hocutt's transcript represented a too gradual approach for some, as this choice ultimately served as the prevailing factor in Hocutt's being denied admittance into the UNC pharmacy program in 1933. Thereafter, some of Shepard's luster among younger blacks began to fade. Shepard was aware of his personal critics and the deteriorating support for Republicans among a segment of the black community, but he remained steadfast in his support for the party. Although many prominent black leaders of the 1930s remained loyal to the Republican Party, Shepard's open advocacy for Republican candidates during the 1930s through the 1940s was unique for a black college president during this era. This was especially distinctive because he faced such harsh criticism from the black community while also remaining the head of a state-supported institution of higher learning in a state where both Democrats and Republicans decided which entities received state appropriations. Therefore, this chapter argues that James E. Shepard placed his uplift strategy of higher education for the black community in North Carolina over that of the national philosophy for racial advancement.[3]

In the spring of 1930 and one year after the stock market crashed, leading the United States into the Great Depression, James Shepard's loyalty to local politicians placed him in direct confrontation with the NAACP. Days prior to his third annual Stock-Taking Conference, Shepard released his public endorsement for John J. Parker's confirmation to the US Supreme Court, although Parker openly supported the disenfranchisement of African Americans. Shepard's endorsement for this controversial judge came in a private letter of congratulations to Parker, which was read at the judge's Senate confirmation hearing. The NCC president's loyalty to this Republican nominee conflicted with the position of the NAACP and a segment of the black community that was tired of the lily-white politics of that party.[4]

In the early 1930s, the NAACP began to shift its political backing to the Democratic Party because the Republicans did not give sufficient support for antilynching legislation. Consequently, Shepard's endorsement for the US Supreme Court of the chief political representative of the lily-white faction of the Republican Party created tension between Parker and the civil rights organization. This strain was caused largely because of John Parker's style of politics. Parker was a North Carolina Republican who stood for women's suffrage during his campaign for governor in 1920. This strategy served him well in the polls, as his Democratic competitor Cameron Morrison was staunchly opposed to women's suffrage at least until the Nineteenth Amendment officially passed. With an influx of newly registered white women voting, Morrison, who had openly opposed the Nineteenth Amendment, now found himself campaigning for this new voting bloc. Ironically, his job was made easier as a vast majority of registered white women voted with their husbands, fathers, and sons by casting their ballots for the Democratic Party. According to Glenda Gilmore, this was largely because historically, the Democratic Party had been viewed as the White Man's Party, and now that white women could vote, it also became the White Woman's Party. Notwithstanding his support for women's suffrage, Parker's affiliation with the Republican Party created the illusion that he represented the working class and minorities. To quell those fears among white North Carolinians, the GOP nominee spoke adamantly against Negro suffrage as a way to appease his white constituencies.[5]

In an attempt to distance himself from black Republicans, Parker argued "the Negro as a class does not desire to enter politics" and "the Republican Party of North Carolina does not desire him to do so." But with the help of a strong force of white women as his campaign aides, Morrison defeated Parker and became governor of North Carolina. Parker's statement that "the Republican Party of North Carolina does not desire [the Negro to vote]" led to heavy scrutiny of his political career by the NAACP.[6]

Although Parker lost the governor's race in 1920, the conservative tactics that he employed in his campaign changed the fabric of the Republican Party both nationally and locally. According to historian Kenneth Goings, Parker's commitment to the lily-white faction of the GOP placed him in high esteem with party leaders. This admiration was certified in 1923 when Parker was appointed special assistant to the attorney general of the United States by Republican president Calvin Coolidge. The Republican Party also displayed its appreciation for Parker's "transformative politics" by electing him as a member of the Republican National Committee in 1924. President Coolidge's respect for Parker was displayed again in 1925, when he nominated the UNC College of Law graduate to the United States Court of Appeals for the Fourth Circuit. The US Senate later confirmed Parker. Despite his political setback in 1920, Parker's career ascended largely due to his stance against the Negro vote.[7]

Ten years after his failed attempt to become the governor of North Carolina, Judge John J. Parker found himself in another political quagmire over his confirmation to the US Supreme Court. This opportunity came about when Associate Justice Edward Terry Sanford died on March 8, 1930, giving Republican president Herbert Hoover the opportunity to appoint someone to the Supreme Court who shared his political and social views. The respect that Hoover had for John Parker was shown in 1929 when Hoover considered appointing him US attorney general. The president eventually decided against this appointment because of concerns raised by one of his advisors about the extent of Parker's knowledge of the law. With the death of Justice Sanford, Hoover considered appointing Parker to the nation's highest court largely due to his "lily white politics."[8]

Judge Parker began a political campaign for the Supreme Court position that rivaled his campaign for governor ten years earlier. This time, however, the judge did not only have to convince white North Carolinians that he was well suited for this position; he also had to convince northern African Americans that he was not a southern white supremacist. The latter task was a tall order and would have been more difficult had he not had a number of prominent black leaders to speak on his behalf. However, African American opposition to Parker's nomination became more stringent as the judge's lily-white rhetoric remained steadfast during his campaign for confirmation.[9]

While remaining loyal to the lily-white roots that helped to advance his political career, John J. Parker's candidacy for the US Supreme Court was furiously challenged by the NAACP. As Walter White, the acting secretary for the NAACP, and other leaders of the civil rights organization issued a frontal assault on Parker's nomination to the Supreme Court, the judge and his advocates reached out to prominent blacks who had ties to the Republican Party for their endorsements. Dr. Robert R. Moton, president of the Tuskegee Institute, received correspondence from Parker's team in hopes that Moton would issue a statement on behalf of their nominee. Parker's campaign committee appeared confident of gaining support from Moton because the Tuskegee president had just been appointed to the Haitian Investigation Committee by President Hoover.[10]

Moton refused to openly support Parker's nomination, however. Parker did not live in Alabama, and it was unlikely that Tuskegee's president would receive pressure from local officials to publicly endorse the judge. Despite his desire to remain silent, Moton's name was invoked during the judge's confirmation hearing. During his hearing before the Senate, the NAACP and Walter White highlighted Parker's stance against black suffrage. But Lee S. Overman, Democratic senator from North Carolina and former trustee of Shepard's school, pointed out that Robert Moton held the same beliefs on black suffrage as John Parker. Although the Tuskegee president did not openly support Parker's nomination, his gradualist stance on the black vote was linked to Parker's antiblack suffrage stance, which in turn created a backlash against Booker T. Washington's successor from the national black media.[11]

After being confronted with the refusal of any prominent southern black leader to speak on Parker's behalf, the judge's campaign team focused its attention on the Tar Heel State. Senator Lee S. Overman seemingly encouraged James E. Shepard to issue his public and private endorsement for the judge. Prior to Parker's nomination becoming so hotly contested by the NAACP, Shepard forwarded the judge a letter of congratulations, which he likely presumed would remain a personal correspondence. But during the judge's confirmation hearing, Overman read Shepard's note in which he emphasized that the NCC president felt that Parker would "be fair to colored people." After Shepard's letter was read to the Senate subcommittee, individuals from both Parker's and the NAACP's camp reached out to Shepard for either confirmation or clarification pertaining to his once private and now public letter of congratulations. Shortly thereafter, Shepard issued a public endorsement of Parker to the national black media. This endorsement from Shepard surprised some within the black community.[12]

In an attempt to calm the racial tension that Parker created with his antiblack suffrage diatribe, Shepard informed the editors of the *Baltimore Afro-American* that he "still believes Judge J. J. Parker, white, fit for the U. S. Supreme Court despite the Judge's public statements" pertaining to the black vote. The black college president proclaimed, "I know his personal friendly attitude to my race and to me." Shepard ended his endorsement by reassuring his constituents that "I believe that if he is elevated to the Supreme Court Bench that the Negro will have no fairer or truer friend."[13]

Shortly after the NCC president issued this statement of support for Parker, the black media swiftly went into attack mode against Shepard. One of Shepard's major media supporters during the infancy of his school, the *Pittsburgh Courier*, was the first to publish a story on the subject. "Our Shepard of Durham," the headline read on April 26, 1930. The attacking article by one of the *Courier's* staff writers initially showed some hesitation. Clearly still holding Shepard in high esteem, the writer stated that "our good brother, James E. Shepard, of Durham, North Carolina, has put himself in the unusual position of challenging, single-handedly, the multiplied judgment of almost all straight-thinking Negroes of this country." Because they considered Shepard's endorsement an "unusual act," they were "going to do the unusual thing and tell him about it." In essence, the editor issued "their Shepard" a subdued tongue-lashing.[14]

The writer then attacked Shepard's endorsement of Parker's nomination. First, the issue of Parker's personal feelings toward the Negro did not concern the *Courier*. "The fact that he expressed himself as opposing certain citizens enjoying their Constitutional rights is all that gave birth to the opposition so strenuously registered against his confirmation." Clearly, the editor did not want Shepard's sentiments of Parker's cordiality toward the race to overshadow his vehement sentiments against the black franchise. Parker's "personal feeling to-ward Negroes had nothing to do with the opposition to Judge Parker any more than his personal feeling toward labor." The writer alluded to the fact that the American Federation of Labor was also opposed to Parker's nomination due to the judge's support of yellow-dog contracts, which awarded mining contracts to individuals who were not members of labor unions.[15]

The tone of the article began to change from a reluctant tongue-lashing to an all-out attack. "In all probability Judge Parker likes Dr. Shepard," speculated the *Courier*. Since Parker and Shepard both resided in North Carolina, the *Courier* figured that the two men had a personal relationship prior to Shepard's controversial endorsement of the judge. "We will even admit that in all probability Judge Parker would lend Dr. Shepard some money and do other personal courtesies for Dr. Shepard." But, as the *Courier's* writers noted, Parker's personal sentiments for one man, or even for the race as a whole, could not overshadow his antiblack position on suffrage. "These personal courtesies extended by Judge Parker to one Negro could never, no never in all the world qualify Judge Parker to sit in judgment on the Constitutional rights of people who, in Judge Parker's opinion, have no business exercising political rights."[16]

The *Courier* then questioned Shepard's loyalty to his race. While understand-ing that he was the head of a state-supported institution, the writer refused to give NCC's president a pass. "Dr. Shepard lives in North Carolina and is the head of a school which depends upon appropriations made by the North Caro-lina Legislature," the writer recalled. "We do not know how much this condition influenced Dr. Shepard, but we do know that Dr. Shepard, in the minds of many intelligent Negroes, displayed himself to the world as a weakling, a deserter of Negro rights, and placed himself in the position to merit the opprobrium of all right-thinking Negroes," the angry attack continued.[17]

In the article's conclusion, the writer issued a final blow to Shepard's character and his standing as a respected black leader. "We are sorry for Dr. Shepard, but when it comes to selecting reliable Negro leaders in the future, we certainly hope the name of Dr. Shepard will be conspicuously absent from the list." In the past, the *Courier* and other black newspapers had listed Shepard as a prominent and effective race leader. In March 1926, Shepard had been on the list of finalists for the Spingarn Medal, an award established by Joel E. Spingarn in 1915 and presented by the NAACP to an African American who reached "the highest and noblest achievement of an American Negro." Now with his support of John J. Parker, the black media was no longer sure if he deserved such recognition.[18]

Shortly after the *Pittsburgh Courier's* attack on Shepard's character, Ben Davis, editor of the *Atlanta Independent*, echoed the *Courier's* sentiments. Davis proclaimed that "a white man's attitude toward his individual Negro is in no sense expressive of his attitude to the Race." That sentiment suggested that Shepard was the property of John Parker. With his reference to Shepard being the personal property of Parker serving as his opening, Davis's rhetoric became even more personal. This time the *Atlanta Independent* editor spoke of black college presidents in general. "As a rule, Negro educators who get their pay from political sources do not represent the highest character and best thought of the race," Davis argued. In an era when more outspoken criticism of the current racial conditions was accepted, individuals like Ben Davis were able to express their disgust for the old style of black leadership more freely.[19]

Davis made it clear that he distrusted the gradualist stance on civil rights. In Davis's mind, proponents of this approach were merely puppets for "the white man," and therefore the time had come for Shepard and other gradualist leaders to step aside. To cement that idea, Davis argued that black educators "cannot escape the tinge of vacillation that confesses automatically the white man's superiority complex." Once again Davis suggested that Shepard and other publicly funded black college presidents had an inferiority complex and therefore should not be trusted. The editor concluded, "Dr. Shepard has not done himself any good with the white folks, and has lessened his usefulness in the regard of his own race." Davis's distrust of black educators also underlines the divide between southern black college presidents and the NAACP. Their agendas of racial advancement were somewhat different by the 1930s, with black colleges focusing largely on creating a prosperous black middle class in the early twentieth century through higher education. The NAACP, on the other hand, focused on larger themes such as eradicating mob violence and providing equal access for the race.[20]

Like the *Pittsburgh Courier*, Davis wished to tarnish Shepard's legacy within the black community due to the latter's support of Judge Parker's nomination to the Supreme Court. In closing, Ben Davis issued his endorsement of the NAACP's battle against Parker's confirmation and strengthened his heated rhetoric against James Shepard. "The Negroes are with the N.A.A.C.P. in its fight for their manhood rights," Davis asserted, "and will pay but little attention to Dr. Shepard, whom they have never heard of before in their behalf." Davis ignored that Shepard was currently preparing to host the third annual Stock-Taking Conference, which addressed issues pertaining to the black farmer. Moreover, Davis wanted to obscure Shepard's outspoken endorsement of the black male franchise in 1900 when Shepard argued that southern white supremacists were "unmanning" the black male by disenfranchising him.[21]

Just four years removed from his nomination for the NAACP's Spingarn Medal and two years after being named president of the Stock-Taking Conference, James Shepard found himself defending his record on racial uplift. Directing his rebuttal to Ben Davis and the editors of the *Pittsburgh Courier*, Shepard argued emphatically, "I am not in politics nor do I play the game of politics." When pressed to explain his relationship with Judge Parker, the black college administrator informed the editors of the *Baltimore Afro-American* that he did not know the judge personally and would not "recognize him if he came into this room." This statement raised concerns as to why Shepard would endorse the controversial Supreme Court nominee against the opposition of the NAACP. Shepard answered "because he is a Republican and because I do not think President Hoover would nominate an unfit person." Shepard had been faithful to the Republican Party since the late nineteenth century. The Republican Party had awarded Shepard two political appointments, as deputy collector for the United States Internal Revenue Service and tax assessor for the state of North Carolina. The party had also been responsible for freeing his parents and millions of other slaves in the mid-nineteenth century. Shepard closed his statement by defending his own character and his emphatic defense of his race, proclaiming, "In every fight for the manhood of my race, I have ever stood with them."[22]

In July 1930, Dr. Simon G. Atkins, president of the state-supported Winston-Salem Teachers College, also endorsed Parker's nomination to the US Supreme

Court. According to the *Chicago Defender*, Atkins endorsed Parker after the Shepard controversy had calmed down. In contrast to Shepard's endorsement months earlier, Atkins was supported by the *Chicago Defender* as being a man "like Shepard" of great judgment and that therefore the black community should support the endorsements of Drs. Shepard and Atkins for Parker's confirmation. This last point illustrates the political climate in which Shepard and other publicly funded black college presidents were surviving. Had Shepard refused to openly endorse Parker's nomination to the Supreme Court, the lily-white dominated state legislature clearly would not have supported Shepard's school, especially during the Depression. By staying in line with the wishes of both the local and national politicians of North Carolina, the Shepard and Atkins endorsements revealed their lack of choice in the matter. Shepard had learned the lessons of political favors years earlier when his school's state funds were saved after being placed in jeopardy because of his failure to remove his hat in the presence of white state legislators.[23]

Months after this controversy died down, two prominent individuals from Durham's black community defended Dr. Shepard's character and his legacy as one of the preeminent leaders of that area. On June 28, 1930, the same paper that just two months earlier had lambasted Shepard for his endorsement of John Parker published an article that defended the president's role as a race leader. Attorney R. McCant Andrews of Durham and Louis E. Austin, editor of the *Carolina Times*, informed Floyd Clavin, editor of the *Pittsburgh Courier,* that although they secured hundreds of affidavits opposing Judge Parker's nomination, they still supported Shepard's leadership in the black community. This outpouring of support for Shepard displayed the nuanced politics practiced by Durham's black community. This vote of confidence on Shepard's behalf also reveals the respect that the NCC president had earned over the past twenty years while creating an institution of higher education for the black community of Durham.[24]

After the Parker controversy was settled, Shepard went back to work for black North Carolinians. In August 1933, Shepard wrote to Secretary of Labor Frances Perkins protesting the actions of some employers who were attempting to secure exemptions from the new minimum wage code. From Shepard's perspective, certain employers were not adhering to the code, which guaranteed a minimum wage for all workers regardless of race. The NCC president informed the secretary of labor that "I have been appraised that numerous merchants and others who employ workers have asked that the generally accepted industrial code do not apply to janitors, elevator operators, porters, and similar workers in public buildings." Clearly, Shepard and Secretary Perkins knew that members of the African American community constituted most of the employees that served in those positions; therefore, not providing a minimum wage to those workers would ultimately damage the black community as a whole. Shepard queried whether Labor Secretary Perkins would "use her great office to see that the forgotten black man does not suffer a discrimination so indefensible as this?" Although it is unclear if Secretary Perkins responded directly to Shepard's appeal for justice on behalf of the black worker, what *is* clear is that by 1936 Perkins, with the support of other New Deal cabinet members such as Harold Ickes, increased the number of African Americans who benefited from New Deal programs. For example, the African American presence in the Civilian Conservation Corps (CCC) gradually increased from the mid-to-late 1930s. This increase gave African Americans the opportunity to serve in supervisory roles in the CCC, which in turn led the CCC to support programs that directly benefited the black community during the Depression.[25]

After a summer in 1933 filled with controversy and at the height of the Great Depression, Shepard found his institution facing a budget shortfall. Shepard felt that he had proven his loyalty to the Republican Party in general and to John J. Parker in particular. Therefore, the black college president reached out to the judge for his support. In October 1933, Shepard sent a note to Judge Parker informing "his new friend" that his institution was now facing a $5,200 shortfall and that the state of North Carolina was not planning on increasing the institution's appropriations. Parker informed Shepard that he would reward his loyalty. "I shall be glad to do more than just merely write a letter to [Governor J. C. B. Ehringhaus]," the judge related. In an expression of his appreciation for Shepard's endorsement and attempting to return the favor, Parker informed the NCC administrator "I shall call on the governor and urge him to do everything that can be done on your behalf."[26]

Knowing the political environment, Shepard kept the pressure on Parker for an endorsement for his institution. "I am quite certain that when you talk with Governor Ehringhaus on Wednesday that you will accomplish something for the Institution," he noted. Shepard further informed Parker that he would send the governor a personal note on the day that Parker was to meet with him in support of the judge's request for funds for NCC. To Shepard's delight, although Judge Parker was unable to meet with the governor personally due to Ehringhaus's travel schedule, the judge did send the governor a letter of support, which Shepard felt would "bear fruit."[27]

Although the state of North Carolina did not increase the appropriations

for NCC for the academic year of 1933–1934, James Shepard's political maneuvering was used to gain largess for his institution and not for his private benefit. Shepard's political strategy during the early 1930s coincided with shrinking
tax revenues, the loss of value in investments, and the stream of philanthropic
donations drying up for all institutions of higher education across the nation.
Shepard was facing a $5,200 shortfall at a time when state legislators were seek-
ing ways to reduce their state budgets. One of the chief proposals for budget cuts
was the dismissal of college and university faculty members. While this may
have proved appealing to lawmakers in terms of their bottom line, such a tactic
was bad for black colleges during the 1930s because 35 percent of them experienced enrollment growth. With more students enrolling in college, the thought
of laying off faculty and staff was counterproductive for these colleges.[28]

Notwithstanding the economic hardship that all institutions of higher education faced during that decade, researcher D. O. W. Holmes argues that black
colleges suffered more than PWCUs because black colleges already had smaller
appropriations. Therefore, Holmes stated, "in the light of small appropriations
[the black college] necessarily suffers more than the white schools with much
larger appropriations." In summation, while Shepard's political posturing may
have appeared to work against the agenda of the NAACP and other leaders in
the national black community, the support or "cover" that he provided southern white lawmakers would eventually pay off for NCC to the tune of more
appropriations.[29]

Notwithstanding the circumstances surrounding his choices, Shepard's critics might argue that the Parker debacle and the Hocutt decision marked the
signature episode of the decade for Shepard. Nevertheless, Shepard faced larger
issues during the 1930s that should not be overlooked. Not only was the country facing the greatest economic disaster in the nation's history, but the 1930s
marked the beginning of a paradigm shift in the way African Americans on
a national level practiced politics. Simply put, a group of African Americans
began to support the Democratic Party while chastising those individuals who
openly supported Republican candidates.

This decade also tested the president's inner strength as one of his best friends
died. In May 1935, Charles H. Shepard, a noted surgeon and brother of James E.
Shepard, passed away from complications of a cerebral hemorrhage. The death
of his brother weighed heavily on James Shepard. Charles was a great surgeon
and was very active in the "civic and religious enterprises in Durham." Following
the death of a sibling, personal ally, and supporter in racial uplift during a time
when his other supporters' backing was waning, James E. Shepard faced the re-

mainder of his life's challenges with the support of a decidedly female coterie of advisors—his five sisters; his mother; his wife; and his two daughters, Marjorie and Annie Day.[30]

Just seven months after the loss of his brother, Shepard once again proved his commitment to the black community and his college in particular by taking the controversial step of asking Dixie governors to oppose lynching. In December 1935, Shepard issued a challenge to southern state governors to "take a stand against lynching and protect prisoners at all costs," which in his mind would "eradicate the evil [of lynching] and thus void the possibility of a Federal anti-mob statute." On the one hand, Shepard's statement was an attack on the idea of a federal anti-mob statute, which would achieve what the president wanted done. That is, it would simply protect the black community from mob violence. "If our Southern governors will take a stand against lynching and protect prisoners at any cost," Shepard proclaimed, "this dreadful evil will soon be eradicated from American life and there will be no need of a federal anti-lynching law on the statute books."[31]

But from Shepard's standpoint, if this bill passed it would simply be another piece of legislation that would go unenforced, while shifting states' funds away from education to create agencies that would potentially eradicate mob violence. These funds in the president's mind could be better spent on black higher education. Therefore, he called for southern governors to stop lynchings before the federal government created a law that would force southern states to supply officers to enforce it. Shepard considered the antilynching bill "unnecessary . . . legislation which even the Federal government is powerless to enforce nor even has the desire to do so." From Shepard's perspective, this point was best underlined by the slow support that the African American community received from New Deal legislation. According to New Deal historians, during Roosevelt's first term in office, many civil rights progressives such as Frances Perkins and Harold Ickes wanted to push more forcefully to have African Americans' needs included in New Deal legislation but feared a southern backlash. FDR's first term was filled with more promise for the black community rather than true, effective legislation. Scholar Kelly Miller argued that the early New Deal was not a good deal for the black community. Moreover, according to Shepard's personal research, more than eighteen lynchings occurred after the congressional filibuster of the Costigan-Wagner antilynching bill of 1935. Therefore, Shepard's argument against federal antilynching legislation was an argument for increased funds for his institution and other black colleges throughout the South as well as for the overall protection of the black community.[32]

Shepard again attacked the NAACP and the Democratic Party by serving as a prominent black voice against a federal antilynching bill. The NAACP and Walter White's desire to pass antilynching legislation dated back to the 1920s; they had some support from Republican legislators for the Dyer Anti-Lynching bill. Sadly, for White and the NAACP, however, they only received a halfhearted show of support from Republicans in the US House of Representatives as well as an unenthusiastic response from Republican president Warren G. Harding. The defeat of the Dyer bill was chiefly attributed to one of Shepard's former college trustees, North Carolina Democratic senator Lee S. Overman, who died in 1930, five years before his political party attempted to push new antilynching legislation. The lack of response from Republican politicians in the 1920s led White in search of a new direction for support in the passage of federal legislation against lynching. This search ended with the NAACP's secretary supporting Franklin Roosevelt for the presidency of the United States. While White and the NAACP had grown tired of the false promises of the GOP, Shepard's ties to local politicians and the national Republican Party, coupled with his constant political maneuvering to maintain and gain additional support for NCC at all costs, led to his stance against the idea of a federal antilynching bill.[33]

This point is best highlighted by evaluating the ability and willingness of the South to appropriately fund public education compared to the ability of the North to do the same in the 1930s. David A. Lane Jr. published an article on this subject in 1930 that detailed the national report on education titled *Federal Relations to Education: A Memorandum of Progress by the National Advisory Committee on Education*. His report found that at the beginning of the Great Depression, southern educators made a strong argument for more federal funds for public education because of dwindling southern tax revenues. The report argued that "the national taxing power of the federal government and the inequalities in wealth from state to state make it imperative that the federal government should give financial aid to education in the states." While this argument was largely being made on the behalf of southern education in general, the report went onto encourage the federal government to allow states to "expand the funds in whatever educational directions they see fit." This terminology was adopted so as to systematically "overlook" black colleges' funding needs. To further that point, southern PWCU presidents praised the evolution of black colleges from the late nineteenth century up to the 1930s and recalled that such growth could not have occurred with the support of state dollars alone. Therefore, they argued that the majority of black colleges should continue to seek funding from philanthropic organizations rather than in the form of federal or state appropriations.[34]

While the majority report was represented by a wide range of PWCU presidents from southern colleges throughout the region, the minority report was compiled by Mordecai Johnson of Howard University, Robert Moton of the Tuskegee Institute, and H. L. Dickason of West Virginia State College. Understanding the economic and political climate that they were operating in but also aware that a number of their PWCU colleagues desired to cut black colleges out of any federal grant opportunity, these black college presidents issued a stern rebuttal. They argued that the federal government had a moral obligation to fund black education and claimed that "the unique financial disadvantages under which the public education of Negroes labors in the Southern and border states" made it necessary for the federal government to fund black colleges.[35]

The minority argument was later strengthened by providing the committee with a brief history lesson. Only seventy years removed from what scholars of the day termed as "The Great American Error (slavery)," the black college presidents desired to reveal the disadvantages that the Negro community still faced during the mid-twentieth century due to the horrors of slavery and its aftermath. Beginning their explanation, the minority report used the same argument as the majority report, proclaiming that currently the South was unable to appropriately fund public education. The black college presidents reminded the nation that the majority of the slaves had lived in the South and that this hideous institution benefited every region in the Union. Attempting to quantify the financial benefit slavery brought to the United States, the minority report argued that "four million Southern slaves, formerly 'property' valued conservatively at two billion dollars, became, overnight, four million citizens of the Southern states of the United States." Nevertheless, in light of the argument for the federal government's role in providing aid for southern education, the minority report proclaimed that "in light of history, education of the Negro, set free and given citizenship by federal decree, was such a national responsibility, a responsibility which has not been discharged." It is important to observe that while this debate between the federal government, southern educators, and southern politicians was ensuing, James Shepard issued his appeal for southern governors to stop lynchings before the federal government passed legislation that would draw funds away from black colleges. Clearly, Shepard was not operating in isolation, as it was likely that his true desire was not to divert the federal government's attention (or funds) away from providing more aid to southern education—especially black education.[36]

One month after Shepard's Dixie governors' appeal, responses from those elected officials began pouring in, with the first coming from the Democratic governor of Virginia, George C. Peery. In an open letter to Shepard, Governor Peery informed the college president that in regard to the crime of lynching, "we have an anti-lynching law in Virginia that was enacted in 1928." He proclaimed, "Since the passage of the law in Virginia we have not had a [documented] lynching in this state." Virginia's governor seemed to be siding with Shepard in the latter's opposition to federal legislation that would affect the way the South was governed. To strengthen Peery's argument, the governor stated "I believe that other states might well consider the advisability in adopting a similar law." Peery emphatically stated, "It is the matter for the states to handle but it should be handled effectively." The last point hints at the argument that Shepard made in terms of the federal government not really desiring to enforce true antilynching legislation. Therefore, according to Peery, it should be considered a state issue.[37]

By February 1936, two more Democratic Dixie governors had responded to Shepard's call to stop lynchings. The first response came from Governor J. C. B. Ehringhaus of North Carolina and the other from J. M. Futrell, governor of Arkansas. Ehringhaus informed Shepard that he "shall try in the future as in the past to do all possible to better the condition and opportunity of each and all of our citizens." J. M. Futrell recalled that he was "opposed to the lynching of any human being." Although these two statements from southern governors were not as strong as the one issued by the Virginia governor, the fact that they even responded to a black college president on the subject of lynching reveals the respect and status that Shepard had gained within the South in the 1930s.[38]

As the winter winds of 1936 changed to the warm breezes of spring, James Shepard's stance on lynching and "Negro rights" became more emphatic. During an interracial conference for social workers that was held at NCC in May 1936, Shepard expressed views on race relations that were contradictory to those painted of him by Ben Davis of the *Atlanta Independent* and the editors of the *Pittsburgh Courier* just three years earlier. Beginning his address by evoking the words of Thomas Jefferson, the college president recalled, "All men are created equal and are endowed by their creator with certain inalienable rights among which are life, liberty and pursuit of happiness." Those rights, Shepard argued, "gave to the common man unprecedented dignity and importance and he dreamed dreams of the future glory of a country committed to such a belief."[39]

In a swift rebuke to one of the Founding Fathers, the black college president said that "these dreams were false dreams, the utterances of Thomas Jefferson, written into the American Declaration of Independence were then and are now, equally as false." The Declaration of Independence was drafted when African Americans were enslaved and that even in the 1930s many of their "inalienable rights" were still missing, Shepard said. He clarified that "it was the expression of an idealist and those who subscribed to the ideals did not themselves intend that the facts should be faced." The black college administrator argued that it was hard for him to believe in the Declaration of Independence when his race lacked voting rights.[40]

Shepard ended his address with an evaluation of the current state of race relations. "When millions are deprived of the right to exercise their suffrage in determining those who shall shape their social, economic and political destiny, then there is no such thinking as those millions sharing in inalienable rights, life, liberty and pursuit of happiness." Three years after being castigated as a race deserter, James Shepard spoke out against the status quo of race relations in the United States. Yet weeks later, the NCC president renewed his commitment to the Republican Party, a party that had long abandoned its original commitment to the African American community due to the party's adoption of lily-white politics.[41]

Shepard faced yet another political challenge in the summer of 1936. With the momentum that Franklin Roosevelt was making in gaining support from the black community with the help of the NAACP, GOP party leaders began looking for answers to stifle that shift. Once again the Party of Lincoln turned to James Shepard for support, largely due to his status in the black community and because of his support of Judge Parker. In the fall elections, 70 percent of the black voters in North Carolina voted for the Democratic Party's national ticket. Republican Party leaders sought to stop the bleeding and turned to the NCC president for campaign assistance.[42]

Dr. Shepard proudly rallied black support for Republican candidates during the 1936 elections. That particular campaign cycle took the NCC administrator as far away as New York City on behalf of GOP nominees. Notwithstanding his loyalty to the party, in personal correspondence he informed party leaders when he felt that a Republican candidate was not the best fit for his race. After the 1936 campaign season was over, Shepard demonstrated his loyalty to the party by not pressing for travel reimbursement, because as the president informed Charles Jones, he "believe[s] that [the Republican Party] is the only hope of the disadvantaged people of this country."[43]

In 1937, one year after Shepard campaigned for Republican candidates around the nation and seven years after publically endorsing John J. Parker's candidacy for the US Supreme Court, his political payday had arrived. Although he did not receive an official cabinet position on the local, state, or federal level, appropriations to North Carolina College increased so significantly that black media sources such as the *Atlanta Daily Word* and the *Cleveland Call and Post* published articles on the subject. Editor Floyd Calvin praised Shepard's success in securing both federal and state appropriations for the expansion of his institution. From Calvin's perspective, Shepard's ability to secure such a large appropriation during the height of the Great Depression was "a rare achievement in the annals of Negro education in the South."[44]

While other institutions of higher education were tightening their budgets during the national economic crisis, Shepard's political maneuvering allowed NCC to expand its faculty and staff by employing personnel with more advanced degrees by the fall of 1937 than in previous years. These new hires had earned graduate degrees from Clark University, Iowa University, The Sorbonne, the University of Washington, Cornell University, and New York University. These new faculty included V. V. Oak, department of commerce; Lottie Penn Kimble, house directress of the girls dormitory; Annie P. Washington, house mother in the boys' dormitory; William Burghardt, director of physical education; John B. McLendon Jr., assistant coach; J. Lucille Jackson, director of home economics; Ralph Mitchell, replacing G. M. Bush, who left to pursue a graduate degree in science at Iowa University; and Alphonse Heninburg, Phi Beta Kappa, French instructor and special assistant to the president.[45]

These hirings also occurred during a building boom at NCC. By December 1937, the attacks against Shepard from individuals in the black community for his earlier political decisions appeared irrelevant as Shepard prepared to dedicate nine new buildings on his campus, which came to a total cost of $291,000. These funds derived from grants from the state of North Carolina and the federal Public Works Administration (PWA). The buildings included the Benjamin Newton Duke Auditorium, a library, six faculty cottages, and a male dormitory. At the dedication ceremony, the praises for Shepard's politics came from black and white friends in both the Democratic and Republican Parties. North Carolina's Democratic governor Clyde Roark Hoey, the individual who actually prepared the bill that authorized the state grants for the erection of Shepard's buildings, served as the keynote speaker. Speaking in the new $76,000 B. N. Duke auditorium, Hoey remarked that "North Carolina believes in education which will develop the dominant possibilities of all citizens, regardless of creed or color."[46]

Frank Porter Graham, a future senator from North Carolina and then president of the University of North Carolina at Chapel Hill (UNC), also addressed the audience. Evoking the spirit of the moment, Graham praised a performance by the NCC chorus singing the "Hallelujah Chorus." Thereafter, the UNC president recalled, "I felt within me the struggle of a great race—the soul and the majesty of a great race on the march for the kingdom of God." Graham's address underscored the Thomas Hocutt case as he noted that the "equality of educational opportunity depended too much upon whether a child is white or colored or upon the section in which he lives." Instead, Graham argued, "Christ taught equality of all, but that day has yet to come."[47]

With Hoey and Graham serving as the opening acts for the dedication ceremony, politicians and educators from around the nation participated in this event. Howard University's Mordecai Johnson, who just seven years earlier had—along with two other black college presidents—prepared a report on the special need for federal aid for black colleges, also spoke at the ceremony. Johnson's address challenged white southerners to continue their support of black education. Continuing with the theme of the minority report on southern education, Johnson informed the audience that "these buildings have been put here through the instrumentality of the legislature of a state which a few years ago held slaves: they have been placed here by the descendants of men, many of whom felt that Negroes could not be educated and that we belonged to an inferior race." Johnson concluded that NCC's buildings "have been put here for the most humble element of the population so that in giving a liberal arts education we might learn the mysteries of world economics, politics and social forces." Recalling the early aims of Shepard's school, Johnson reminded the standing room only crowd that these buildings represented "the profound significance of the Christian religion and the Democratic significance of faith in God."[48]

Continuing in line with Johnson's sentiments, Robert P. Daniel, president of Shaw University (Shepard's alma mater), argued that public and private southern education should work together. Using the southern pastime of football as a metaphor, Daniel argued that "the private schools [were] the offensive lines and the state schools [were the running backs]." Placing the private schools on the offensive line likely symbolized the idea that private colleges were the most important factors in the development of southern education. Nevertheless, keeping with the football metaphor of the fans cheering for the ball carriers and not the blockers, Daniel viewed the state schools as receiving larger praise for producing the bulk of the middle class, and thus garnering more funds. But in order to have a winning football program, one needs to have a solid signal caller, and Daniel argued that Shepard should be that man. "I'd like to put N. C. State at the quarterback post," Daniel proclaimed, "because Dr. Shepard, through his long experience, knows when to hit the line or to make an end run around the legislature." That last remark hints at the political decisions Shepard had made for the well-being of his institution throughout his tenure as president and that other black college presidents understood and respected "his game plan."[49]

As the 1930s marked the beginning of a paradigm shift in the United States on a number of fronts, including how African Americans demanded political and civil rights—direct protest was favored by the younger generation as opposed to the more methodical tactics of the previous one—James E. Shepard's legacy at NCC and in the black community of North Carolina in general was cemented. Although many of the decisions that the black college president made during that decade were unpopular within the black community, Shepard's loyalty to the institutions that he believed would advance his race can never be debated. A lifelong Republican, Shepard constantly endorsed GOP candidates despite the opposition of the NAACP and other "radical" African Americans. That blind support caused a harsh backlash from the black community. A black leader seemingly standing in the way of the progress that the NAACP was making for the race baffled many African Americans. However, from Shepard's standpoint, the Republican Party and its candidates were a better option for the black community than Democratic nominees; therefore, he publicly and privately went on record saying so. The spoils from Shepard's political strategy benefited NCC. Shepard did not lobby GOP leaders, Republican senators, or Republican congressmen for personal political appointments that would advance his own status in the national spotlight after he became president of his institution. Shepard's payoff for his political maneuvering was support for his school, which in turn from his standpoint would benefit the entire race.

6

"Don't Crash the Gate but Stand on Your Own Feet!"

Shepard and His Legacy

Still relishing the euphoria that came with the increased state appropriations he received in 1937, James E. Shepard, president of the North Carolina College for Negroes (NCC), could finally feel that his legacy as an advocate for his race was solidified. But his gradualist stance on civil rights was again about to be challenged. This new confrontation mirrored the Thomas Hocutt case of 1933 but with more sophistication. Just months after the National Association for the Advancement of Colored People's (NAACP) chief attorneys, Charles Houston and William Hastie, claimed victory in gaining access for African Americans to professional and graduate schools in the state of Missouri with the *Missouri ex rel Gaines v. Canada* case, the state of North Carolina braced itself for a similar challenge. In *Missouri*, Houston and Hastie were able to effectively argue that the state was not adhering to the Fourteenth Amendment of the United States Constitution because it did not provide equal access for blacks to obtain professional or graduate education within the state. The US Supreme Court therefore decided in December 1938 to order Missouri to provide equal access in professional and graduate schools for African Americans within the state of Missouri.[1]

This new, more nuanced case for integration challenged Shepard and other black college presidents. Once again they were forced to fight against the NAACP's integrationist agenda. White counterparts, such as Frank Porter Graham, president of the University of North Carolina at Chapel Hill (UNC), the state's flagship institution of higher education, were exonerated by some for their gradual stance on civil rights issues because "as a state employee Graham had sworn to uphold both the U.S. Constitution and the North Carolina Constitution." Some radical African Americans and liberal whites judged Graham not for his gradual approach to integration but by the support that he gave the black community in ways that did not break state or federal law.

Shepard, on the other hand, was judged differently. His role as a state employee was not considered when he chose to eschew a radical stance on civil rights issues. Although Shepard was able to capitalize on the *Gaines* case by expanding NCC into a graduate school, his status as a proponent of racial uplift was again challenged as some radical blacks argued that he and other black college presidents placed the needs of their institutions over the needs of the entire race.[2]

Shortly after the *Gaines* decision, Pauli Murray, a young North Carolina expatriate, chose to test the constitutionality of segregated professional and graduate education in North Carolina. Murray was aware that after the *Gaines* decision, black college presidents throughout the nation would attempt to capitalize on the fear of integrated education by asking for funding to create law, pharmacy, and medical colleges at their institutions. Rather than apply for admission into one of the aforementioned programs at UNC, Murray went the unconventional route of requesting to apply for graduate study in sociology there. Recalling the Thomas Hocutt case, Murray did not want Dr. Shepard to serve as a barrier in her application process. Therefore, she attempted to use her family's lineage to influence James Shepard to support her application for graduate education at UNC.[3]

Murray wrote NCC's president a note that seemingly served as a reintroduction. Desiring to establish her credibility with the man responsible for Thomas Hocutt's not gaining admittance into the UNC pharmacy program, Murray carefully crafted her note. First, she reminded Shepard that her grandfather, Robert G. Fitzgerald, was one of the first black educators in the state after Reconstruction. This point was likely made because Shepard viewed education as a vessel for racial uplift. Second, wanting to strongly reestablish a connection with Dr. Shepard, Murray recalled "my aunt and adopted mother, Mrs. Pauline F. Dame, has been a teacher in the Durham City Schools for some decades." The point was important for multiple reasons. Murray already understood that her mother and Shepard shared a good relationship prior to her attempts to integrate UNC. Shepard and Dame also shared a professional relationship as he had served as the president of the North Carolina Teachers Association. Surely, his responsibility as an advocate for Dame and other black teachers in North Carolina would cause Shepard to stand with Murray, as Murray hoped.[4]

Murray then informed Shepard of her intention to integrate UNC. Aware of the largesse that Shepard received for his political maneuvering in the 1930s, Murray probably assumed that Shepard would move to ask the state for funds to create professional programs at his institution. She also knew that state government officials as well as Frank Porter Graham would support him. To that point, Murray wrote that "setting up separate graduate schools merely continues the double standard of education." Murray furthered the argument of the NAACP that separate education established a double standard, thus rendering black institutions ill equipped to fully train the African American community. According to their argument, building graduate programs at black colleges did not uphold the *Gaines* decision to the fullest extent of the law, as African Americans were still not being afforded equal access to professional and graduate education.[5]

Murray waited for the NCC president's response, a reply that did not come. Murray wrote another letter to Shepard, this time closing with the address of the *Carolina Times*, conspicuously located at the end of the note. Recalling the backlash that he received from the black media after the John J. Parker debacle, Shepard wanted to head off any negative press that would likely mount should this correspondence be leaked. So he quickly replied to Murray's second letter. He remained neutral on the issue of her desire to integrate UNC. This was clearly a road that Shepard did not want to travel down, especially after surviving the difficult decade of the 1930s that included the Hocutt and Parker situations. Shepard also understood that Murray's stand on integration was more radical than his, so he chose not to support her cause.[6]

One year prior to his correspondence with Murray, Shepard—when asked by the editors of the *New Journal and Guide* for best practices in obtaining a job— was as shrewd as ever. "Do not try to use influence to get yourself on payroll," the NCC president stated, speaking volumes as to why he likely "overlooked" Murray's first note. Not only would an enthusiastic partnership with Murray strain his relationships with state, federal, and educational officials, but also, from Shepard's perspective, using personal relationships to advance one's cause "shows that you are trying to 'crash the gate' and that you haven't the backbone to stand on your own feet." Murray was yearning to "crash the gate" of segregated education; however, Shepard's analysis was slightly off in this instance as Murray also showed a willingness to "stand on her own feet" in her attempts to integrate the UNC system. Also, for Shepard this was a bit of a contradiction, as he had used personal relationships to build his institution into the respected college that it was.[7]

As Murray predicted, Shepard, with the support of Governor Clyde Hoey and Frank Graham, pursued the creation of a pharmacy school at NCC, which opened in 1940. In an attempt to maintain segregated education during the mid-1940s, NCC's operating expense budget became the fourth largest in the state, behind only the three consolidated colleges in the UNC system. Shepard, as well as his colleagues at Duke and UNC, championed these state funds.[8]

To gain support for his graduate programs, Shepard made a strong appeal to the Carnegie Foundation. On November 6, 1940, the NCC administrator sent a seven-page letter outlining the practicality and need of graduate education at his institution to Dr. Frederick P. Keppel, president of the Carnegie Corporation. The first argument that the black college president used was likely the college's greatest asset: its location. Shepard stated that the strategic location of his institution was "hardly equaled by any other institution of higher learning for Negroes in the Nation." It had close proximity to two of the most respected southern PWCUs in the nation, and Durham was close to Atlanta and Washington, DC, both locations with large black populations that had premier undergraduate black colleges. Rather than continue to send black students north to receive graduate and professional education, NCC could serve as a hub for southern black professional development. This would uphold the *Gaines* decision, and it would also bring NCC closer to its sister schools in Durham and Chapel Hill. The graduate programs at NCC were in full operation by the mid-1940s, with the colleges of pharmacy and law coming on line in 1940 and a graduate program in library sciences in 1941.[9]

While still grappling with the best way to capitalize on the *Gaines* decision, Shepard received an honor that represented the respect he earned in North Carolina. The Reverend William Arthur Cooper of Charlotte set out to create oil portraits of the one hundred most influential black leaders in North Carolina, including James Shepard. It was no surprise to many when Rev. Cooper chose Shepard's image along with seven others to inaugurate the Gallery of Negro Leaders. The other notables included Charles C. Spaulding, president of the North Carolina Mutual Life Insurance Company; Dr. Charlotte Hawkins Brown, president of Palmer Memorial Institute in Greensboro; Ezekiel E. Smith, founding president of the State Negro Normal School in Fayetteville; Dr. G. E. Davis, executive secretary of the state teachers' association; Dr. Simon G. Atkins, founding president of Winston-Salem State College; and Mrs. Annie W. Holland, former state supervisor of elementary schools.[10]

This honor coincided with Murray's and the NAACP's attempts to integrate the UNC system. Although Shepard was granted extra provisions to create graduate programs in 1939, the Murray case still lingered. Desiring to counter Murray's struggle to gain graduate admittance into the UNC Department of Sociology, Shepard, with the support of Frank Graham, created yet another obstacle for Murray by hiring Guy B. Johnson. Johnson, a renowned sociology professor at UNC, was no stranger to black colleges as he worked closely with black college faculty from Atlanta University, Fisk University, and the Tuskegee Institute, documenting sociological data pertaining to black colleges. The professor's connections with black colleges went further still as he also served as a trustee for Howard University, making his selection as a faculty member in Shepard's sociology department a perfect fit. Johnson's assignment of responsibility called for him to teach a course in social anthropology in the spring quarter of 1943, an assignment that he looked forward to fulfilling.[11]

Shortly after the *Gaines* decision, Johnson performed a study on the reactions of southern states to the ruling. "Have Negroes been admitted into white schools?" was the first question on the survey, with specific graduate and professional programs having their own categories. With the exception of Maryland and West Virginia, Johnson found that no PWCU in the South admitted an African American into their school at the undergraduate level. On the other hand, Mississippi, North Carolina, and Texas provided in-state opportunities for African Americans to obtain professional or graduate education. According to Johnson's study, the state of North Carolina had created law, engineering, graduate studies, and library science programs for African Americans by 1939.[12]

Another important finding of this study was the aid that southern states provided African Americans seeking graduate education in northern institutions had increased in each southern state. According to the *Gaines* decision, states were mandated to provide in-state graduate and professional education to all state citizens regardless of race. Johnson's study found that the majority of southern states still operated in the same manner that they had prior to the Supreme Court decision in 1938.[13]

Johnson's appointment at NCC had two effects. It served as a barrier for Murray by maintaining segregated education in North Carolina and also provided Johnson with access to more black students, which would grant him a greater understanding of what black college students truly desired in terms of civil rights. After conducting a series of studies pertaining to this subject, Johnson drew the conclusion that the South was weighing itself down by not providing African Americans with adequate educational opportunities. He ultimately advanced an argument of W. E. B. Du Bois that if African Americans did not have proper educations, the South would become economically stagnated. From these scholars' perspective, the South could only rise as high as an educated work force would allow it. Therefore, the denial of proper education for black southerners was not only a civil rights violation; it was also detrimental to southern economic viability.[14]

Murray's attempt to integrate higher education in North Carolina coincided with the beginning of World War II. Prominent black scholars such as Howard University's chair of history, Rayford Logan, continuously worked to highlight racism at home and abroad during the war. For example, in 1940, the same year that Shepard's pharmacy and law programs opened, Logan testified before Congress on behalf of the Committee on the Participation of Negroes in the National Defense. In his testimony, the World War I veteran argued that African Americans demanded "equal opportunity to participate in the national-defense program, civil as well as military." With Logan's outspoken demands for black participation in national defense programs and the emergence of African American support for the Double V campaign, Shepard's gradual approach to racial advancement seemed too conservative to many in the black community.[15]

In 1944 James Shepard issued a plea of his own before the US House of Representatives. Unlike Logan's call for racial equality, Shepard's cry aimed at gaining financial support for the war. Only a few years removed from the grips of the Great Depression, Shepard took the unusual stance of asking the representatives for increasing general sales taxes for 1944. According to Shepard, such a measure would "reach the surplus buying power and at the same time every person [would be] conscious of his individual daily financial support of the war effort and the benefits of American citizenship." From Shepard's perspective, increasing the sales tax not only would make the American citizens who were fighting and dying in World War II be active participants in defeating the Axis powers, but all American citizens would play a functioning part in that potential victory.[16]

Although the idea of shared responsibility was fitting for some, others argued that such a measure during a war and a weak economy would be disastrous. The counterargument to Shepard's appeal was clear and concise. White-collar individuals would be unable to expand the economy by hiring more employees with money they saved from not having the new sales tax. Poor citizens would simply be unable to afford the new levy. Working-class citizens would make as few purchases as possible, ultimately making the idea of a new sales tax unprofitable. Shepard contended that a sales tax was the fairest way to spread the financial burden of war. The black college president also argued that a sales tax would not burden "the fixed income groups, whose salaries' have not been raised appreciably during the past few years, because these persons had never been extravagate spenders." Shepard further reminded the representatives that individuals of the fixed-income groups were "the savers of the country" and "we never had to worry about savers." In his final push for patriotism, the college administrator recalled that "while it is true that poor people would be contributing their 'widow's mite' it would be done cheerfully because of the many benefits we are now receiving." Shepard understood that the price of freedom was sacrifice, and therefore, he believed that this cost should be shared by the entire nation, both elite and proletariat. At the close of his address, Representatives Robert L. Doughton of North Carolina and Harold Knukcey of Minnesota congratulated Shepard.[17]

For African Americans who supported the Double V campaign, Shepard's argument was unconscionable. First, the argument for a sales tax appeared unjust as this type of levy was regressive. In essence, poor African Americans would financially contribute a higher percentage of their income than wealthy whites under Shepard's plan. From their perspective, if the president wanted to have a reasonable levy, he should have made an argument for an income tax. That way, the elites (both white and black) would carry more of the financial burden for the war as citizens would only be taxed on their earnings rather than their expenditures. Second, the college president's action reminded many in the black community of Joe Louis's generosity to the federal government in January of 1942. This act of kindness came after the "Brown Bomber" defeated Buddie Baer and then donated his winnings to the war effort. After that incident, many in the black community refused to applaud the champ's patriotism because in their minds these funds supported a segregated military system. To juxtapose that image, the NAACP awarded attorney William Hastie the Spingarn Medal in March of 1943 for resigning as a civilian aide to the secretary of war because of the government's stance on segregation in the United States military. Therefore, Shepard's position on a shared responsibility went against the grain of black politics by the war years.[18]

On February 17, 1944, Shepard was invited to the Blue Network radio station in New York City to participate in a town hall meeting titled "Let's Face the Race Question." Participants in this forum were both liberal and conservative, white and black. All were nationally respected for the works they had done in their respective fields. For example, editor, author, and poet Langston Hughes and former California commissioner of immigration in California, Carey Mc-Williams, made the case that the race problem should be attacked nationally with the support of the federal government. Keeping with his stance in support of states' rights, Shepard, along with John Temple Graves II, editor of the *Birmingham Age-Herald,* made the argument that "the problem of obtaining full citizenship privileges and opportunities for Negroes should be left in the hands of state and community authorities."[19]

After this national forum, the attacks that Shepard received from some members of the black community resembled those heaped upon him after the John J. Parker debacle. "There Ought To Be A Federal Law," read the headlines of the *Chicago Defender* on February 26. Attacking Shepard and Graves's argument of states' rights, the *Defender* explained that states' rights "has always been used as a potent weapon against progress." Highlighting the southerners' argument, the *Defender* recalled that Shepard and Graves's gradual approach would eventually be detrimental because the Jim Crow system was always evolving. The newspaper recalled the damning statistics that Carey McWilliams produced during the meeting. "The Mississippi State Senate is putting new teeth in the Jim Crow laws," the writer proclaimed, "by voting to impose a penalty of $50 on common carriers for failure to keep passengers segregated by race." The *Defender* noted that the previous fine for such a violation was only $25. From its perspective, this was a clear example of the South being unable to legislate fairly in terms of racial equality.[20]

Although the *Defender's* criticism of Shepard's view of race relations was more tempered than what he received from the black media in the early 1930s, Ben Davis's critique was not. Davis, editor of the *Atlanta Daily World*, was one of the chief media adversaries of Shepard during the latter's support of Parker. When NCC's president argued on behalf of states' rights, Davis responded with disdain. "As We Expected," his editorial began. Davis was supported by Louis Austin, editor of the *Carolina Times*, in his attack on Shepard. After the Parker debacle, Austin had written an article in support of Shepard's leadership in North Carolina, while Davis and the editors of the *Pittsburgh Courier* challenged the NCC president's status as a trusted Negro leader. This time, however, Davis informed his readers that even Austin viewed Shepard's race position as "embarrassing and contrary to the thinking of the majority of Negroes of North Carolina."[21]

With extreme passion, Louis Austin not only attacked Shepard's argument that the state of North Carolina was a perfect example of gradualism; he also attacked his "elite" status. The *Carolina Times* editor argued that Shepard and others of the North Carolina black elite were out of step with the masses of their race. Moreover, he asserted, these Negro leaders were making decisions in their own best interest and not in the interest of the people. Austin argued that many black leaders were too cozy with the white establishment; therefore, it was hard for these leaders to take tough stances against their "white friends."[22]

In closing, Austin fully endorsed Langston Hughes's view of racial advancement while also issuing a warning to Shepard's white supporters. "The speech delivered by Dr. Shepard at Town Hall, and that delivered by Langston Hughes, present two opposite views of a very important question," Austin recalled. "It would be appalling to many white persons in this state to know the loss of respect which Dr. Shepard incurred among those of his own race to deliver that speech." While Shepard's respect amongst black North Carolinians declined, Langston Hughes' status ascended because of his "courageous utterance on the same program."[23]

After more than two months of stinging criticism, Shepard wanted to recast his approach to the race question. During the 32nd annual North Carolina Conference for Social Services held in Raleigh, Shepard argued that it was the duty of whites to end discrimination. "The Negro believes that the task of the white man in America is to see that discrimination" ends, Shepard recalled. The NCC president wanted to see the demise of racial discrimination in "war industry, governmental bureaus and agencies." Angered by attacks on his integrity and loyalty to his race, Shepard took this opportunity to clarify his views.[24]

"Negroes should have economic freedom, justice in the courts, equal teachers' salaries and the right to sit on juries," he argued. Contradicting Louis Austin's portrayal of him as an aloof elite, Shepard vehemently opposed the efforts of southern states to extend the Jim Crow laws in public facilities. The college administrator also made a passionate plea for black suffrage. "Opportunity to exercise the right and obligation to vote and perform other duties incumbent upon full citizenship of the United States should be guaranteed to all citizens," he declared.[25]

Finally, Shepard issued a public reprimand. Recalling that the Tar Heel State had imperfect race relations, the president nevertheless argued that the progress made there was due to its "democratic and Christian" concepts of dealing with the race problem. While praising the individuals that continually funded his institution, Shepard condemned the "white supremacy legislature" and the city of "Richmond, Kentucky; Fenton B. Sands of New York City, N.Y; Harold E. Ward of Flint, Mich.; Flight Officers; Edward S. Pressly, Chicago Ill.; Wendell R. Smith, Des Monies [sic], Ia.; and Alphonse C. Toler, Bluefield, W. Va." The *Atlanta Daily World* praised this address for showing "unprecedented courage for a state school administrator."[26]

As the head of an institution that relied on state and federal funds for survival, James Shepard could not be as continuously vocal as Rayford Logan and Langston Hughes on the issue of racial injustice. He could, however, use his institution as a platform to highlight the issues of racial inequality. Therefore, in the late spring of 1944, with the support of Nathan Carter Newbold, the super-

visor of Negro education in North Carolina, James Shepard initiated a conference on race relations at NCC. With Newbold's support, Shepard reached out
to prominent white and black North Carolinians to make presentations at his
summit on race, which was scheduled for July.[27]

One of the first individuals whom Newbold targeted for this conference
was Frank Graham, who was initially scheduled to address the issue of race
relations in the nation. After some careful consideration, however, Shepard
decided that Graham was better suited to discuss views of race relations in
North Carolina from the perspective of a white person. Other individuals
and topics scheduled for the conference covered the spectrum of American
life. For example, Dr. Clyde A. Erwin, the state superintendent of public instruction, discussed public education and race relations, while Dr. John Hope
Franklin, professor of history at NCC, discussed industry and race relations in
North Carolina. Although this conference was slated to address the problems
of racial relations in North Carolina in a pragmatic manner in order to create
a more civil society, Shepard found that the emotions of race outweighed the
desire for cooperation.[28]

During his presentation, members of the crowd heckled Graham as they
clearly disapproved of his opinion that race relations in North Carolina would
improve through religious means. These individuals were no longer responsive
to the calls that things would get better due to prayer and "the great by and by."
This was obviously not the outcome that James Shepard hoped for, especially
since the anger was directed toward someone who served as a political ally.[29]

Days later, Shepard forwarded Graham a note of apology. "It is rather discon-
certing to a man who seeks to do right as he sees it to be continually 'heckled'
by people of smaller minds and no sense of social justice." Being a man of faith
himself, Shepard encouraged Graham not to lose his confidence in humanity or
the "eternal verities of God." He finished his note to Graham by encouraging him
in his belief that his religiosity and liberal values would prevail. "You represent a
symbol of truth and liberty," Shepard asserted, "and these principles will eventually prevail for they are eternal." Prior to closing this brief letter, NCC's administrator assured the UNC president that he still had a friend and supporter in Durham, despite the negative reaction that Graham received during his address.[30]

Feeling reassured that he had not lost the support of a friend in Shepard,
Graham responded to the NCC administrator. "I wish to thank you for your
letter," Graham wrote. "It meant much to me to be in conference with you the
other day." The UNC president was delighted that Shepard personally reached
out to him after his address. He also appreciated that his colleague agreed

with his assessment of improving race relations. Graham's sentiments reflected some of the same views that Shepard had expressed during his address at 32nd annual North Carolina Conference for Social Services.[31]

Although Graham understood the sentiments of the hecklers, he felt that more progressive dialogue needed to occur. Staying true to his Christian character, Graham attacked his cynics' analysis of his address. "In this complex and difficult area all of us need not only the wise processes of education," the UNC president cautioned, "but the enduring resources of religion." Notwithstanding his frayed feelings toward his critics, Graham ended his note to Shepard "with warm personal regards always." Graham obviously did not hold Shepard personally accountable for the actions of some of the conference attendees.[32]

Shepard would again call on his UNC colleague for support regarding a racially sensitive matter. With the war drawing to a close, African American veterans were returning home with a new outlook on life. They believed that if they could be asked to risk their lives for the freedoms of individuals in foreign countries, then their own freedoms should be expanded back home. However, many white southerners pressed back against the new mentality of these returning soldiers. When black veterans breached the code of southern racial etiquette, some white southerners reminded these "Negroes" of their place through public humiliation, violence, and even murder. This was the case in Durham during the summer of 1944, when Homer Lee Council, a white public bus driver, murdered Booker T. Spicely, a black veteran, for ignoring the Jim Crow laws.[33]

Booker Thomas Spicely was born on December 1, 1909, to Lazarus and Alberta Spicely in Blackstone, Virginia. Spicely had been briefly employed as the assistant business manager of the Tuskegee Institute. He joined the United States Army on December 31, 1943, weeks after his thirty-fourth birthday. Spicely was skilled as a cook, a job that was not uncommon for an African American who enlisted in the military in the mid-twentieth century. Once Spicely earned the rank of private in the army, he was stationed in Camp Butner, North Carolina, only fifteen miles away from Durham. After witnessing the segregated conditions of the military and experiencing the vicissitudes that came with being an African American in the army, Spicely's yearning for respect engulfed him.[34]

In the early days of July and during the heat of a southern summer, Private Spicely was awarded a rest and relaxation pass. Wanting to reorient himself with the black community, Spicely made the quick journey to Durham. Sadly, neither his uniform nor the black citizens of Durham could protect him from the racial customs that were ingrained in everyday life.[35]

On July 8, 1944, Spicely sat at a local bus stop. In full uniform, Private Spicely encountered a black family that was also awaiting the arrival of the bus. After a few minutes, the family expressed their appreciation for Spicely's service and the pride they had for an African American in uniform. This conversation likely boosted the private's confidence as his next course of action was irrational, especially in the Jim Crow South. Upon the arrival of their bus, Spicely and the family boarded. Unlike the local family that moved to the rear of the bus, Spicely occupied the first open seat. This space was in the whites-only section. The white bus driver, Homer Lee Council, demanded that Spicely move to the rear of the bus. Spicely fired back at the driver that he was a man in uniform and deserved to sit wherever he wanted too. The black family that had waited with Spicely at the bus stop begged him to move to the Jim Crow section but to no avail.[36]

The driver came to another stop where white soldiers boarded the bus. These soldiers also pleaded with Spicely to move. After making his stand, Spicely decided that he would get off the bus at the next stop. When the bus approached that stop, Spicely disembarked, perhaps thinking he had gained some respect by refusing to comply with the segregated policy of this transportation company. What Spicely did not know, however, was how far Homer Council was willing to go to ensure that the Jim Crow laws would not be violated.[37]

After Spicely left the bus, Council disembarked as well. When Spicely turned around to speak to the enraged driver, Council fired two shots in the private's chest. Spicely died immediately due to the two gunshot wounds, one through his heart and one through his liver. With this public act of violence, Homer Council could not conceal that he was the murderer of a US soldier. Therefore, many in the black community felt that the Spicely family and the black community in general would get justice.[38]

Black citizens cried for justice throughout the community of Durham, the state of North Carolina, and the nation. Understanding the racial and political climate that loomed in the aftermath of the Spicely murder, North Carolina governor J. Melville Broughton asked Durham's black leaders to lead the way in this case. The governor wanted to keep the NAACP's attorneys away from the case as he likely felt that their presence would lead to a racial uprising. Once again, James Shepard came to the state government's rescue by keeping the NAACP's legal team away. With the support of other local black leaders such as Charles C. Spaulding, Shepard initiated a local legal campaign to have Homer Council convicted of first-degree murder.[39]

After months of planning, Shepard, with the support of the black leadership of Durham, began lobbying for funds to prosecute Homer Council. By the fall of 1944 and months after his summit on race relations, Shepard called on some of the same individuals who had attended the conference for support in the Council-Spicely case. One of the first appeal letters went to his UNC colleague, Frank Graham. After a series of meetings discussing the appropriate direction of the case, Graham, Shepard, and Spaulding agreed to raise a total of $500 for the case. On September 1, Shepard informed UNC's president that the committee had agreed on the services of a local attorney to prosecute the case. "Will you go ahead and raise the amount which you agreed to do," Shepard asked his Chapel Hill neighbor, "and send your check to Mr. C. C. Spaulding whom I have directed to act as treasurer."[40]

This case highlighted the partnership that Shepard had developed between black and white business and community leaders in Durham and the surrounding areas. It also shows his leadership skills and the respect he garnered from those individuals as he had the ability to "direct" C. C. Spaulding to act as treasurer for this cause. Spaulding was one of the most revered leaders in North Carolina during the mid-twentieth century. Nevertheless, time and again, this businessman forfeited leadership positions to Shepard when they worked together on specific causes, such as the Stock-Taking conference and now the Council-Spicely case.[41]

Frank Graham went to the black community of Chapel Hill for donations. By September 20, James Shepard reported to N. C. Newbold that the group had only raised $177.50 for the attorney. According to Shepard, he and Spaulding raised $150 while Graham had been successful in raising $27.50. Desiring to place some pressure on the supervisor of Negro education, Shepard encouraged Newbold to help raise the remaining funds from liberal whites who resided in Raleigh. Shepard knew that his legacy rested on his ability to raise these funds. Over the previous three decades, Shepard had gained a reputation as a man who was able to generate funds for his causes regardless of the economic climate. Therefore, he knew he could not fail in this racially sensitive venture, especially since he would be held responsible for not allowing the NAACP to openly support this case.[42]

Just five days after reporting that he had collected more than $27 in Chapel Hill, Frank Graham informed Shepard that more money was coming. He sent a check for $50 from Dr. Howard Odum, chair of the sociology department of UNC. Graham also informed his colleague in Durham that the Chapel Hill contingent would be able to donate more than $100 for the "fund of defense and fair justice for all citizens." Moreover, he issued a challenge to Shepard and N. C. Newbold to double the amount of money that was raised in the small village of Chapel Hill.[43]

According to Spaulding, by October 14, the committee had collected $525 for the prosecution of Homer Council, with the largest donation coming from James Shepard, who donated more than $52 of his own money. Despite this show of support across racial lines in central North Carolina, Council was able to escape first-degree murder charges. Instead of facing life in prison, he was charged with second-degree murder, only to have that sentence overturned. The defense argued that Council was simply defending himself and through this act of self-defense, Spicely died. Once again a cloud of uncertainty loomed over Shepard and the black leaders of Durham as their efforts to have Council prosecuted failed. These individuals felt betrayed by the governor after this verdict because he had promised a fair trial. They also had to prepare themselves to answer tough questions pertaining to the effectiveness of their leadership after this ruling.[44]

With the loss of the Council-Spicely case burning in the memories of black North Carolinians, Shepard perhaps anticipated yet another round of attacks from the black press. But during the spring of 1945, members of the national black media polled their readers as to "Who is Our National Leader?" James E. Shepard emerged as the people's choice for black leadership. Of the twenty-three national leaders on the list, Shepard received 782,500 votes in this poll. Other individuals receiving substantial votes were: C. C. Spaulding, 646,000; Dr. Mordecai W. Johnson, president of Howard University, 602,000; and Asa Philip Randolph, Brotherhood of Sleeping Car Porters, 544,500.[45]

After learning that he had been selected as the "national leader of his race," the seventy-year-old Shepard became more vocal on racial matters. The first example of his new outspokenness came in the winter of 1946 as he talked of the plight of the Negro in North Carolina. During an address on a North Carolina radio broadcast, Shepard informed his audience that the majority of African Americans in the Tar Heel State lived in houses that were "unfit for human habitation." Desiring to show health care discrepancies between the white and black communities, Shepard informed the listeners "for every 6,499 Negroes in the state, there is only one physician." Compared to one doctor for every 1,127 white persons. From Shepard's perspective, these conditions were clearly caused by the "dixie system of segregation and prejudice."[46]

With a new degree of confidence, Shepard moved to his criticism to the US military. He recalled that North Carolina "stood at the top of the list of all the 48 states in the percentage of men who were rejected from military services" because of illiteracy or poor health. This was unlike the president's normal approach to discussing racial issues. Usually, he highlighted the great advances that were occurring in the Tar Heel State while pointing to the disadvantages that "Negroes" of other states faced.[47]

While somewhat free in expressing his opinions of racial inequalities in North Carolina, Shepard was mindful that his address could have been viewed as radical. Therefore, he closed his interview by shielding the governor from sharp criticism. Recalling a case where a young African American male was sentenced to death for a "heinous crime," the president stated, "Governor [Gregg] Cherry is commuting the death penalty of a young Negro." Shepard informed his listeners that Cherry felt compelled not to see the youth killed because the state had failed him by not providing the young man a fair chance at the American Dream.[48]

In the midst of Shepard's new outspokenness, NCC had become one of the finest southern institutions of higher learning for African Americans. His legacy as the founding president of NCC was honored during the spring commencement of 1946, when more than 120 of his students received degrees. During the ceremonies, the audience that filled the B. N. Duke auditorium was treated to a dramatic depiction of the life and works of Dr. Shepard. This was likely a very special moment for the president as he was able to view the struggles that he had experienced while creating his institutions through the portrayals of his students and historian Helen G. Edmonds. Surrounded by his wife, Annie Day, his two daughters, Marjorie and Annie Day, and his mother, Hattie, this was one of the last moments of recognition that Shepard was able to fully enjoy.[49]

In 1947, after working with her husband for over thirty-six years to build NCC, Annie Day Shepard died in early February. Locally known for the support she gave her husband in creating and sustaining NCC, the news of her passing not only hurt her immediate family but also her extended NCC family. Annie Day's work for NCC was so respected by her husband that he named a girls' dormitory in her honor. When he heard of Mrs. Shepard's passing, Langston Hughes recalled, "I missed her warm welcome, her sweet smile, and the glow of her lovely white hair." The loss of his wife shook the seventy-one-year-old Shepard to his core. Shepard's mourning was not long-lived before another member of his inner circle was "called home."[50]

On April 18, only six days after celebrating her eighty-eighth birthday, Hattie E. Shepard died. Hattie was remembered as a loyal and devoted servant to the White Rock Baptist Church. After the death of her husband Augustus, Hattie remained active in the church that Augustus pastored by serving as a Sunday school teacher and president of the Women's Home Mission Society.

Speakers at her memorial service were people who knew her both as Mother Shepard and as Dr. Shepard's mother. With the passing of his mother coming only two months after the death of his wife, James's personal health also began to decline.[51]

James Shepard tried to remain strong for his daughters and his NCC family. He did the only thing that he knew: focus his total attention on the continued evolution of his institution. Not satisfied with the great success of his school, Shepard issued a call in the spring of 1947 for the training of more doctors and dentists, as well as the creation of more black hospitals in the state of North Carolina. In yet another radio address, the NCC administrator stated that "some fair and equitable arrangements" should be made so that Negroes would have the opportunity to acquire medical training. Making a similar argument to the one that Pauli Murray made in the late 1930s for greater access in graduate and professional education, Shepard made a strong push for the creation of a medical program at NCC. "Negroes have not had the tools with which to work, the tools with which to improve their living conditions, the tools with which to improve their way of life." Shepard urged the state to provide a better distribution of funds and that those monies be spent on the creation and maintenance of better hospitals and the creation of facilities for the training of doctors and dentists for the "Negro group."[52]

After years of a conservative approach to racial uplift, particularly as it pertained to his school, Shepard's aggressive tone may have appeared more radical to some. For others, "Shepard's new voice," resembled his style prior to his becoming a college president. Although his criticisms of local and state officials were uncommon, the events that surrounded his outspokenness best explain his new position on the race question.

Not only were African American soldiers returning from the battlefields of World War II with a new mindset in terms of black advancement in the United States, but also the federal government on some level began to recognize how egregious the Jim Crow laws were. For example, on December 6, 1946, President Harry S. Truman created a committee of prominent black and white Americans that included Frank Porter Graham to inquire on the condition of civil rights and make recommendations for their improvements. These individuals were then to present a report, which would be titled *To Secure These Rights*, to the president so that he then would be able to make appropriate decisions pertaining to civil rights for African Americans. The researchers for this presidential report were to find answers to the following questions: "1, What is the historic civil rights goal of the American people? 2, In what ways does our present record fall short of the goal? 3, What is government's responsibility for the achievement of the goal? 4, What further steps does the nation now need to take to reach the goal?" Once the report was complete, the research compiled a 178-page document that simply stated that African Americans were being denied their civil rights. Consequently, Truman's civil rights commission argued that the federal government should fight for the "elimination of segregation, based on race, color, creed, or national origin, from American life." Shortly after this report was released, President Truman appointed another interracial committee to investigate segregation in higher education. Soon thereafter, he called for the elimination of discriminatory practices in higher education altogether.[53]

With the changing political environment in terms of the nation's perspective of civil rights, it appears that James Shepard's new approach to the race question was in line with the majority of American citizens. He took the opportunity to speak more emphatically for his race with the understanding that liberal whites would protect him in his new approach. Also, the NCC president capitalized on the White House's interest in civil rights by displaying health discrepancies between the races more forcefully. By doing this, Shepard hoped that the state of North Carolina and other southern states would not only better fund black colleges but create more professional programs at their schools. Therefore, by the spring of 1947 he was making the argument for the creation of black hospitals and black medical programs, which would, in his mind, eliminate discriminatory practices in the medical field. Shepard's "new voice" was an encouraging sign for those individuals who had grown tired of his gradual approach to the race question. He, along with other local black leaders, was displaying the inequalities of the Jim Crow Era, a tactic that younger black radicals had demanded for decades.

Epilogue

A Legacy Continued

The Eagle is no common, ordinary barnyard fowl.
And while a sparrow clings to its flock, an eagle soars alone!

Dr. James E. Shepard

Through the summer of 1947, James Shepard continued to lobby state officials for the creation of a medical program at NCC. Nevertheless, the burden of such a task for the seventy-one-year-old, coupled with the recent deaths of his wife and mother earlier in the year, was a struggle that the president could not overcome. On October 6, 1947, James E. Shepard died of a cerebral hemorrhage weeks before his seventy-second-birthday. Word of his death shocked those in the Durham community as many viewed Shepard as their leader, friend, and family member.[1]

The funeral for Durham's Shepard occurred at the institution that he built in the B. N. Duke Auditorium, named for one of the earliest benefactors of his school. The services for the fallen leader resembled those for the passing of other national icons, as "high state and government officials" traveled to NCC to pay their last respects to Shepard. In his remarks, Gregg Cherry, North Carolina's governor, proclaimed "North Carolina was the home-front on which Dr. Shepard labored unceasingly in racial and educational matters—and his efforts brought definite results." Shortly after his death, James Shepard received one of the greatest endorsements for his approach to racial uplift.[2]

On November 1, 1947, Morehouse College's president, Dr. Benjamin Elijah Mays, wrote an article titled "Jim Shepard." Recalling the conservative leadership of Shepard, Mays observed that "some people criticized Doctor Shepard in his racial philosophy." However, the Morehouse president wrote, "Many people who criticized [Dr. Shepard] severely will never do as much for education and America as he did." Mays recalled the struggles that Shepard had in creating his school in 1910 and then explained with glee how quickly that small training school grew into one of the finest colleges in America. "The growth of the North Carolina College was so rapid," Mays recalled, "that it almost made one dizzy to observe it."[3]

Being a college administrator himself, Mays attempted to give the readers an understanding of Shepard's approach to racial uplift: "I think he took the position that if education in North Carolina had to be segregated, the segregated North Carolina College at Durham would have to be so good that no one would be able to label it as a Negro institution." The Morehouse administrator argued "Dr. Shepard insisted that the State should be willing to pay for its segregation and pay dearly by building a first-class institution." The words of Dr. Mays should have caused many of Shepard's critics to pause and consider the true legacy of the man. From Mays's perspective, it could no longer be argued that Dr. Shepard was not a race man. The mere existence of his publicly funded liberal arts black college in the South stood as a representation of his true and lasting legacy.[4]

Nearly three months after Shepard's death, questions arose as to who would replace the founder and only president of NCC. Prior to making this selection, members of the NCC's board of trustees pondered the direction they wanted to see the college take. They knew that the selection of NCC's second president would be very important in sustaining the success that Shepard had achieved in more than thirty years of service. With Shepard's legacy looming, the trustees' decision appeared more difficult. After much deliberation, the committee decided on a list of finalists for the presidency, a list that comprised only current NCC employees. These individuals were Alfonso Elder, dean of graduate education; Ruth Dean, dean of women; Albert E. Manley, dean of the College of Arts and Sciences; Albert L. Turner, dean of the law school; and James T. Taylor, chief of the Veterans Administration Guidance Center. When asked why a national candidate did not emerge on the list of finalists, the trustees informed the media that they wanted to replace Shepard with someone who was familiar with their fallen leader's vision.[5]

After conducting several interviews with the finalists, Dr. Alfonso Elder, a native of Saundersville, Georgia, was elected as the second president of NCC on January 20, 1948. After completing undergraduate studies at Atlanta University, Elder received his master's and doctoral degrees from Columbia University. Further indicating his erudition is that Elder received additional training from the University of Chicago and the University of Cambridge in England. Prior to arriving in Durham, Elder taught mathematics at Bennett College in Greensboro, North Carolina, from 1921 until 1922; then he accepted a similar position at Elizabeth City State Teachers College from 1922 to 1923. In 1924 Elder came to NCC as a professor of mathematics, a position that he held until 1943. In 1943 Elder accepted the position as dean of the graduate school at Atlanta University, a post that he held until September 1947, when James Shepard offered him a similar position at NCC.[6]

Less than one month into his presidency, Elder delivered his first public address. Understanding the great responsibility that was being bestowed upon him and knowing that he was chosen to keep James Shepard's vision alive, Elder presented his dreams for NCC's future. First the new president wanted to show that he and Shepard shared leadership styles. While revealing Shepard's approach to leadership, Elder recalled that Shepard led with a "deep sense of humility." "Those of you who knew the inner man," the new president recalled, "recognized and appreciated the depth of his character." Elder asserted that Shepard was friendly and that "he was interested in helping people solve their problems, however large or small." In his final analysis of Shepard, Elder believed that the former president "was motivated through a deep religious feeling." These were all the values that Elder felt "should [be] cherish[ed] and foster[ed]" at NCC during his administration.[7]

By the spring of 1949, Shepard's legacy was larger than ever as the institution that he founded began to gain still added recognition under the college's new administration. According to the *Durham Sun*, by March 1949 Elder was preparing to expand NCC's infrastructure with the hopes of making it one of the elite liberal arts institutions in the nation. These plans included the building of

> a music and fine arts building, a modern gymnasium, the surfacing of streets boarding the library building, a domestic science building, two dormitories, a classroom building, an apartment house for teachers, a home economics practice cottage, an infirmary, the installation of a fire protection system for the campus and a central heating plant.[8]

Elder felt that with this expansion, the students of NCC would have adequate facilities that would allow them to grow mentally and thus become productive citizens. Moreover, this plan would also "allow the admission of hundreds of knowledge-hungry students who were refused admission each year." Keeping with Shepard's vision and expanding on it, Elder found his institution in a very prosperous condition one year into his administration. For example, in 1949 NCC enrolled 1,036 students, owned 28 buildings that were valued at approximately $3 million, and employed 2,143 faculty and staff members.[9]

Also, Elder inherited an institution that was a member of the Association of American Colleges, the Association of Colleges and Secondary Schools for Negroes, and the American Council of Education. Importantly, NCC received a class A rating from the American Medical Association, the North Carolina State Department of Education, and the Southern Association of Colleges and Secondary Schools. This rating was important because it certified that NCC's students were eligible to apply for graduate education at institutions that were members of the aforementioned associations, which included the vast majority of PWCUs in the South.[10]

Although expanding NCC's infrastructure served as a chief goal for Elder, Shepard's mission of moral education remained a prominent theme under the new administration. As the editor of a local daily put it, Elder, "like Dr. Shepard has a primary interest in the development of manhood and womanhood among North Carolina College students as well as young people everywhere." Elder, however, also brought with him a new style of leadership that was quite different from the dictatorial style of management for which Shepard was known. A local writer noted that the new president endeared himself to the entire college community through "his belief in democratic administration and genuine respect for the unique worth of every individual." Therefore, with Shepard's vision and Elder's more friendly leadership style, the NCC community's excitement soared.[11]

With Elder gearing up to expand NCC, Shepard's legacy received a glowing tribute from the state legislature of North Carolina. On February 17, 1949, the North Carolina house and senate passed a joint resolution in commemoration of Shepard's legacy. Representative Robert M. Gantt of Durham offered the resolution commending Shepard's services to the state by describing Shepard as "greater than Booker T. Washington." This point was likely made because many local and national political figures still believed that the model of black education and racial uplift was Washington's approach. Nevertheless, according to Representative Gantt, Shepard's uplift and educational strategy in North Carolina were superior to Washington's.[12]

Representative Gantt's sentiments were only the precursor to the flood of praises that were heaped upon Shepard during this ceremony. Shortly after Gantt's address, Representative John W. Umstead praised Shepard for the manner in which he handled race relations. In return for Shepard's conservative style, Umstead recalled that "of all those coming before the appropriations committee he was the only one I got a real pleasure from." Keeping with these sentiments, the resolution honoring Shepard revealed the respect that the former president earned from the legislators while displaying an appreciation for his willingness to hold firm on his gradual approach to racial uplift.[13]

"Whereas, standing as he did in the midst of strong currents and cross currents of conflicting theories and interest," the resolution read, "this man pos-
sessed that peculiar combination of persistence and tact, courage and discre-
tion." The resolution went on to explain the legislators' appreciation for such
courage and tact as they argued that these attributes allowed Shepard to "guide
his people steadily along the slow path of progress, where one false step to the
right or the left might well have spelled disaster."[14]

One of the most powerful passages in this resolution honoring Shepard
spoke directly to the vicissitudes that he faced during his presidency. "Whereas,
while constantly subjected to pressure from sources within and without this
state," recalled the resolution, "and often beset by the forces of ignorance and
actual ill-will, this man kept his mind clear and his vision unclouded." This last
point highlights the struggles that Shepard faced, especially as it related to the
Thomas Hocutt and Pauli Murray cases. In summation, the state legislators of
North Carolina on February 17, 1949, certified that Shepard's works in building
his institution during an era of strong racial feelings should never be forgotten
and always honored.[15]

From 1910 until his death in 1947, James Edward Shepard labored in the
creation of an institution of higher education that he envisioned would usher
black North Carolinians into the twentieth century. Along the way on his thirty-
seven-year journey, Shepard, through his position as a black college president,
found himself in the middle of many racially sensitive issues. The first came in
1900, years before he became president of the NRTIC. That year, virtually every
black male in the Tar Heel State was disenfranchised with the use of Jim Crow
laws. Consequently, a young James Shepard spoke out against the disenfranchisement of these black men. After 1910, however, Shepard's outspoken attacks
against Jim Crow customs were less common, although his struggle to defeat Jim
Crow never yielded.

After a thorough evaluation of his life, one will find it difficult to argue that
Shepard was not working to help elevate his race in the early twentieth century.
Although on many key civil rights issues of the 1930s and 1940s that directly
attacked the segregation of higher education, Shepard appeared to side with
white supremacists. From Shepard's perspective and those of other black college
presidents of the era like Morehouse College's president, Dr. Benjamin E. Mays,
Shepard felt that his institution and other black colleges, if funded properly,
were better suited to educate young black scholars than PWCUs.

If the growth of the black middle class is considered one of the standards
of success for the civil rights movement, James E. Shepard and a host of other

southern black college presidents should gain acclamation for their role in helping to create that class. Importantly, black colleges of the early to late twentieth
century were as responsible for the growth of the black professional class as
any civil rights organization in America. Throughout Shepard's presidency, he
hosted forums on the proper way to advance the black community. Shortly after
many of these meetings, he would assess the findings and implement programs
that addressed the concerns of the platform guest. For example, after the first
Stock-Taking and Fact Finding conference in 1928, Shepard created a school of
business administration to address the need of black-owned businesses in the
black community.

Moreover, James E. Shepard's approach to racial advancement through NCC
mirrored Booker T. Washington's approach to a small degree. Ironically, many
scholars have labeled both men as accommodationists for positions that they
held on key issues as it related to the black community. Although Shepard's and
Washington's educational philosophies were different, their approaches to racial
advancement were similar—their approaches both focused on racial self-help.
These presidents continually fought in the midst of the Jim Crow Era to keep
the doors of their institutions open while working with local, state, and federal agencies to validate the very existence of their programs. Nevertheless, the
schools that they created were producing black professionals who were in turn
returning to the black community as educators, artisans, preachers, and so on.
Simply, these schools and presidents helped to create the southern black professional class despite the attacks they received from southern white supremacists
and black radicals. Finally, the institutions in which Shepard, Washington, and a
host of other southern black college presidents labored during the Jim Crow Era
stand in the twenty-first century as the continued legacy of the men and women
who fought valiantly during the early twentieth century.

After Shepard's death in 1947, the North Carolina College for Negroes continued to flourish through the duration of the twentieth century. One proud moment that Shepard would have surely enjoyed occurred under the school's fourth
president, Dr. Albert N. Whiting. In 1969 Shepard's vision of NCC gaining full
graduate status came to fruition when the name of the school was officially
changed to the North Carolina Central University (NCCU). Forty-one years
later, on July 5, 2010, NCCU celebrated 100 years of existence operating under
the motto that Shepard would surely be very proud of—"Truth and Service."

Notes

Abbreviations

B. N. Duke Papers   Benjamin Newton Duke Papers, David M. Rubenstein Rare Book &
Manuscript Library, Duke University

Du Bois Papers   W. E. B. Du Bois Papers, Ned R. McWherter Library, University of
Memphis

Graham Papers   Frank Porter Graham Papers #1819, Southern Historical Collection, The
Wilson Library, University of North Carolina at Chapel Hill

Hemphill Papers   Hemphill Family Papers, David M. Rubenstein Rare Book &
Manuscript Library, Duke University

Johnson Papers   Guy Benton Johnson Papers #3826, Southern Historical Collection, The
Wilson Library, University of North Carolina at Chapel Hill

Stagg Papers   James E. Stagg Papers, David M. Rubenstein Rare Book & Manuscript
Library, Duke University

Introduction

1. Louis Harlan, *Booker T. Washington: The Wizard of Tuskegee, 1901–1915* (Oxford: University of Oxford Press, 1983); Booker T. Washington, *Up From Slavery: An Autobiography* (New York: Random House, 1999); Robert Norrell, *Up From History: The Life of Booker T. Washington* (Cambridge, MA: Harvard University Press, 2009); W. E. B. Du Bois, *The Souls of Black Folk* (New York: Random House, 1996); David Levering Lewis, *W. E. B. Du Bois: Biography of A Race, 1868–1919* (New York: Henry Holt, 1993); Deborah Gray White, *Too Heavy a Load: Black Women in Defense of Themselves: 1894–1994* (London: W. W. Norton, 1999), 21–56.

2. James D. Anderson, *The Education of Blacks in the South, 1860–1935* (Chapel Hill: University of North Carolina Press, 1988), 48–56; David H. Jackson Jr., "Booker T. Washington's Tour of the Sunshine State, March 1912," *Florida Historical Quarterly* 81 (Winter 2003): 254–78; Amilcar Shabazz, *Advancing Democracy: African Americans and the Struggle for Access and Equity in Higher Education in Texas* (Chapel Hill: University of North Carolina Press, 2004), 1–25.

3. Anderson, *Education of Blacks in the South*; Joe M. Richardson, *A History of Fisk University, 1865–1946* (Tuscaloosa: University of Alabama Press, 1980); James L. Leloudis, *Schooling the New South: Pedagogy, Self and Society in North Carolina, 1882–1920* (Chapel Hill: University of North Carolina Press, 1996).

4. Leroy Davis, *A Clashing of the Soul: John Hope and the Dilemma of African American Leadership and Black Higher Education in the Early Twentieth Century* (Athens: University of Georgia Press, 1998); John Hope Franklin, *Mirror to America: The Autobiography of John Hope Franklin* (New York: Farrar, Straus and Giroux, 2006).

5. J. A. Whitted, *Biographical Sketch of the Life and Work of the Late Rev. Augustus Sheppard, D.D. Durham North Carolina* (Raleigh, NC: Edwards and Broughton Printing, 1912).

6. Ibid.

7. Blair L. M. Kelley, *Right to Ride: Streetcar Boycotts and African American Citizenship in the Era of Plessy v. Ferguson* (Chapel Hill: University of North Carolina Press, 2012), 1–12.

8. Rudyard Kipling, "The White Man's Burden: The United States and the Philippine Islands," *New York Sun*, February 10, 1899.

9. Kevin Gaines, *Uplifting the Race: Black Leadership, Politics, and Culture in the Twentieth Century* (Chapel Hill: University of North Carolina Press, 1996).

10. David Sehat, "The Civilizing Mission of Booker T. Washington," *Journal of Southern History* 73, no. 2 (May 2007): 1–30; Booker T. Washington, "The Colored Ministry: Its Defects and Needs," *The Christian Union*, August 14, 1890; Louis R. Harlan, "Booker T. Washington and the White Man's Burden," *American Historical Review* 71, no. 2 (January 1966): 441–67.

11. Kevin Gaines, *Uplifting the Race: Black Leadership, Politics, and Culture in the Twentieth Century* (Chapel Hill: University of North Carolina Press, 1996); Willard B. Gatewood, *Aristocrats of Color: The Black Elite, 1880–1920* (Bloomington: Indiana University Press, 1990); Glenda Gilmore, *Gender and Jim Crow: Women and the Politics of White Supremacy in North Carolina, 1896–1920* (Chapel Hill: University of North Carolina Press, 1996).

12. Gaines, *Uplifting the Race*; Stephanie Shaw, *What A Woman Ought to Be and Do: Black Professional Women Workers During the Jim Crow Era* (Chicago: University of Chicago Press, 1996); Glenda Gilmore, *Gender and Jim Crow: Women and the Politics of White Supremacy in North Carolina, 1896–1920* (Chapel Hill: University of North Carolina Press, 1996); Gertrude Woodruff Marlowe, *A Right Worthy Grand Mission: Maggie Lena Walker and the Quest for Black Economic Empowerment* (Washington, D.C.: Howard University Press, 2003).

13. Kelley, *Right to Ride*, 3–5.

14. David H. Jackson Jr.'s, "Booker T. Washington's Tour of the Sunshine State, March 1912," and Pero Gaglo Dagbovie, "Exploring A Century Of Historical Scholarship On Booker T. Washington," *Journal of African American History* 92 (2007): 239–64.

15. Glenda Elizabeth Gilmore, *Defying Dixie: The Radical Roots of Civil Rights, 1919–1950* (New York: W. W. Norton, 2008), 265–64. David H. Jackson Jr., *Booker T. Washington and the Struggle Against White Supremacy: The Southern Educational Tours* (New York: Palgrave McMillan, 2008); Christina Greene, *Our Separate Ways: Women and the Black Freedom Movement in Durham, North Carolina* (Chapel Hill: University of North Carolina Press, 2005).

16. Gerald Smith, *A Black Educator in the Segregated South*; L. Davis, *A Clashing of the Soul*; Benjamin E. Mays, *Born to Rebel: An Autobiography*; and Antonio Holland, *Nathan B. Young and the Struggle Over Black Higher Education* and George F. Bagby's "Hollis F. Price: Apprenticeship at Tuskegee," *Alabama Review* 60 (2007): 29–52; Booker T. Gardner, "The Educational Contributions of Booker T. Washington," *The Journal of Negro Education* 44 (1975): 502–18; and Reginald Ellis' "Nathan B. Young: Florida A&M College's Second President and

His Relationship with White Public Officials," in *Go Sound the Trumpet! Selections in Florida's African American History*, E. Canter Brown and David H. Jackson Jr. eds. (Tampa: The University of Tampa Press, 2005), 153–72.

Chapter 1. The Emergence of a Black Leader during the Age of Jim Crow and Black Racial Uplift in North Carolina

1. Eric Foner, *A Short History of Reconstruction: 1863–1877* (New York: Harper and Row, 1990), 238–54; Glenda Elizabeth Gilmore's *Gender and Jim Crow: Women and the Politics of White Supremacy in North Carolina, 1896–1920* (Chapel Hill: University of North Carolina Press, 1996), Thomas Dixon, *The Leopard's Spots: A Romance of the White Man's Burden* (New York: Doubleday and Page, 1902).

2. J. A. Whitted, *Biographical Sketch of the Life and Work of the Late Rev. Augustus Shepard, D.D., Durham, North Carolina* (Raleigh: Edwards and Broughton Printing Company, 1912), 11.

3. Whitted, *Biographical Sketch of Rev. Augustus Shepard*, 25; Todd L. Savitt, "The Education of Physicians at Shaw University, 1882–1918: Problems of Quality and Quantity," in Jeffrey Crow and Flora J. Hatley eds., *Black Americans in North Carolina and the South* (Chapel Hill: University of North Carolina Press, 1984), 160–88.

4. Howard N. Rabinowitz, "A Comparative Perspective on Race Relations in Southern and Northern Cities 1860–1900, with Special Emphasis on Raleigh," in Jeffrey Crow and Flora J. Hatley eds., *Black Americans in North Carolina and the South* (Chapel Hill: University of North Carolina Press, 1984), 137–59.

5. Whitted, *Biographical Sketch of Rev. Augustus Shepard*, 14–15.

6. Ibid., 20.

7. Jacquelyn Rouse, *Lugenia Burns Hope, Black Southern Reformer* (Athens: University of Georgia Press, 1989).

8. Jane Dailey, "Deference and Violence in the Postbellum Urban South: Manners and Massacres in Danville, Virginia," *The Journal of Southern History* 88, no. 3 (August 1997): 556.

9. Booker T. Washington, *Up From Slavery: An Autobiography* (New York: Modern Library, 1999), 143–45; W. E. B. Du Bois, *The Souls of Black Folk* (New York: Penguin, 1989), 36–50.

10. Du Bois, *The Souls of Black Folk*. Interview with Dr. John Hope Franklin and the author, December 17, 2007, Durham, North Carolina, the notes of this interview are in the possession of the author. Dr. Franklin recalled that black citizens of Durham marveled at Shepard's stature, proclaiming, "this is Dr. Shepard's school," every time they passed NCC.

11. Robert F. Durden, *The Dukes of Durham: 1865–1929* (Durham: Duke University Press, 1975), 116–17; Darlene Clark Hine, William C. Hine, and Stanley Harrold, *The African American Odyssey* (Upper Saddle River, New Jersey: Pearson, 2008), 362–63.

12. Hine, Hine, and Harrold, *The African American Odyssey*, 362–63; David Cecelski, *Democracy Betrayed: The Wilmington Race Riot of 1898 and its Legacy* (Chapel Hill: University of North Carolina Press, 1998).

13. James E. Shepard, *Morning Post* (Raleigh, N.C.), January 2, 1900, in Gilmore, *Gender and Jim Crow*, 120; C. Vann Woodward, *The Strange Career of Jim Crow* (Oxford: Oxford University Press, 1974).

14. Deborah Gray White, *Too Heavy A Load: Black Women in Defense of Themselves*,

1894–1994 (New York: W. W. Norton, 1999), 19–20; Evelyn Brooks Higginbotham, *Righteous Discontent: The Women's Movement in the Black Baptist Church, 1880–1920* (Cambridge, MA: Harvard University Press, 1993), 88–119.

15. William J. Kennedy Jr., *The North Carolina Mutual Story: A Symbol of Progress, 1890–1970* (Durham: North Carolina Mutual Life Insurance Company, 1970), i–iv.

16. Ibid., vii.

17. Ibid., 4.

18. Anne S. Butler, "Black Fraternal and Benevolent Societies in Nineteenth-Century America," in Tamara L. Brown, Gregory S. Parks, and Clarenda M. Phillips, eds., *African American Fraternities and Sororities: The Legacy and the Vision* (Lexington: University of Kentucky Press, 2005), 70.

19. Kennedy, *North Carolina Mutual*, 9.

20. George W. Reid, "James E. Shepard and the Public Record of the Founding of North Carolina College At Durham: 1909–1948," in *Negro History Bulletin* 41, no. 6: 900.

21. Robert F. Durden, *The Dukes of Durham: 1865–1929* (Durham, NC: Duke University Press, 1987), 11–25.

22. James E. Shepard to James E. Stagg, March 20, 1899, Stagg Papers.

23. Durden, *Dukes of Durham*, 69; James E. Shepard to James E. Stagg, June 7, 1899, Stagg Papers.

24. James E. Shepard to Benjamin Newton Duke, August 13, 1902, B. N. Duke Papers; James E. Shepard to James Stagg, October 18, 1904, Stagg Papers.

25. James E. Shepard to Benjamin Newton Duke, August 11, 1902, B. N. Duke Papers. The author has not discovered such a letter from Duke on behalf of Shepard, but it is likely that Duke heeded this request as Shepard eventually became superintendent of the ISSA, a decision that was likely influenced by a letter of recommendation from Benjamin Newton Duke.

26. Durden, *Dukes of Durham*, 83.

27. Gilmore, *Gender and Jim Crow*, 79–80.

Chapter 2. "Change the Man and the Environments Will Be Changed by Man": The Creation of the National Religious Training Institution and Chautauqua for the Negro Race

Epigraph source: W. E. B. Du Bois, *The Education of Black People: Ten Critiques, 1906–1960*, ed. Herbert Aptheker (New York: Monthly Review Press, 1973), 77; this was also quoted in Ronald E. Butchart's article titled "Outthinking and Outflanking the Owners of the World": A Historiography of the African American Struggle for Education," *History of Education Quarterly* 28, no. 3 (Autumn, 1988): 333–36.

1. James E. Shepard to Benjamin Newton Duke, April 22, 1908, B. N. Duke Papers. Refer to chapter one for the author's definition of the term racial uplift/uplifting the race.

2. Deborah Gray White, *Aren't I a Woman: Female Slaves in the Plantation South* (New York: W. W. Norton, 1985); Steven Hahn, *A Nation Under Our Feet: Black Political Struggle in The Rural South From Slavery to the Great Migration* (Cambridge, MA: Harvard University Press, 2003); James D. Anderson, *The Education of Blacks in the South, 1860–1935* (Chapel Hill: University of North Carolina Press, 1988), 5; Joe M. Richardson, *Christian Reconstruction:*

The American Missionary Association and Southern Blacks, 1861–1890 (Athens: University of Georgia Press 1996).

3. Amilcar Shabazz, *Advancing Democracy: African Americans and the Struggle for Access and Equity in Higher Education in Texas* (Chapel Hill: University of North Carolina Press, 2004); Anderson, *Education of Blacks in the South*, 33–78.

4. Anderson, *Education of Blacks in the South*, 33–78; Eric Foner, *Reconstruction: America's Unfinished Revolution* (New York: Harper and Row, 1988).

5. Louis Harlan, *Booker T. Washington: The Wizard of Tuskegee, 1901–1915* (Oxford: University of Oxford Press, 1983); Booker T. Washington, *Up From Slavery: An Autobiography* (New York: Random House, 1999); W. E. B. Du Bois, *The Souls of Black Folk* (New York: Random House, 1996); David Levering Lewis, *W. E. B. Du Bois: Biography of A Race, 1868–1919* (New York: Henry Holt, 1993); Gray White, *Too Heavy a Load: Black Women in Defense of Themselves: 1894–1994* (London: W. W. Norton, 1999), 21–56.

6. Lewis, *W. E. B. Du Bois: Biography of A Race*.

7. Louis Harlan, *Booker T. Washington: The Wizard of Tuskegee* (Oxford: University of Oxford Press, 1983), 104–5.

8. Tom Lutz and Susanna Ashton, eds., *These "Colored" United States: African American Essays from the 1920s* (New Brunswick, N.J.: Rutgers University Press, 1996), 212–17; National Training School and Chautauqua Bulletin, 1909, B. N. Duke Papers; Reginald Ellis, "Nathan B. Young: Florida A&M College's Second President and His Relationships with White Public Officials," in *Go Sound the Trumpet!: Selections in Florida's African American History*, ed. Canter Brown Jr. and David H. Jackson Jr., 163 (Tampa, FL: University of Tampa Press, 2005).

9. National Training School and Chautauqua Bulletin, March, 1909, B. N. Duke Papers. Refer to Chapter One of this manuscript to gain a deeper understanding of the author's historical synopsis of the "civilizing mission" along with "racial uplift."

10. Ibid.

11. Theodore Roosevelt to James E. Shepard, December 18, 1908, John C. Kilgo Records and Papers, Duke University Archives, David M. Rubenstein Rare Book & Manuscript Library, Duke University.

12. Ibid., 80–85; Cassandra Tate, *Cigarette Wars: The Triumph of "The Little White Slaver"* (Oxford: Oxford University Press, 1999), 11–37.

13. Tate, *Cigarette Wars*, 11–37.

14. Robert F. Durden, *The Dukes of Durham, 1865–1929* (Durham, NC: Duke University Press, 1975), 83–85, 250.

15. Ibid., 101.

16. James E. Shepard to Benjamin N. Duke, October 3, 1908, B. N. Duke Papers.

17. James E. Shepard to Benjamin Newton Duke, March 6, 1908, B. N. Duke Papers.

18. Ibid., It has not been ascertained if this meeting between the two gentlemen actually occurred once Shepard arrived in New York.

19. Letter Head of the National Religious Training School and Chautauqua for the Colored Race, 1909 (housed in the North Carolina Central Archives).

20. Ibid.; *Afro-America*, October 15, 1910, 6.

21. Letter Head of NRTIC; W.E.B. Du Bois spoke of M.C.B. Mason's esteem as a model moral religious leader in an article on the black church in *The Crisis*, May 1912.

22. Letter Head of NRTIC; Senator Lee S. Overman Papers #570, Southern Historical Collection, The Wilson Library, University of North Carolina at Chapel Hill, finding aid; William B. Hixson Jr., "Moorfield Storey and the Defense of the Dyer Anti-Lynching Bill," *New England Quarterly* 42, no. 1 (March 1969): 65–81. Glenda Gilmore, *Gender and Jim Crow* (Chapel Hill: University of North Carolina Press, 1996), 31–91. *Pittsburgh Courier*, December 14, 1935, 5.

23. James E. Shepard to Benjamin N. Duke, September 22, 1909, B. N. Duke Papers; Robert F. Durden, *The Dukes of Durham, 1865–1929* (Durham, NC: Duke University Press, 1975), 97.

24. James E. Shepard to James Sprunt, October 18, 1909, Alexander Sprunt and Son Records, David M. Rubenstein Rare Book & Manuscript Library, Duke University.

25. James E. Shepard to James Sprunt, November 19, 1909, ibid.

26. James E. Shepard to B. N. Duke, January 19, 1909, B. N. Duke Papers; Stephanie J. Shaw, *What a Woman Ought to Be and to Do: Black Professional Women Workers During the Jim Crow Era* (Chicago: University of Chicago Press, 1996).

27. James E. Shepard to B. N. Duke, January 19, 1910, B. N. Duke Papers.

28. James E. Shepard to B. N. Duke, February 14, 1910, B. N. Duke Papers; On this stationery, Shepard's title under the Advisory Board was president-elect.

29. Durden, *Dukes of Durham*, 91–93.

30. Ibid.

31. *Chicago Defender*, July 23, 1910.

32. Ibid.; *Afro-American*, October 15, 1910.

Chapter 3. Creating an Intellectual Partnership While Easing the White Man's Burden: James E. Shepard Advancing the Race through His Intellectual Partnerships

Epigraph sources: David H. Jackson Jr., *Booker T. Washington and the Struggle Against White Supremacy: The Southern Educational Tours* (New York: Palgrave McMillan, 2008), 168; Benjamin E. Mays, *Born to Rebel: An Autobiography* (Athens: University of Georgia Press, 2003), 196.

1. Jackson, *Booker T. Washington and the Struggle Against White Supremacy*; William H. Lewis "An Account of Washington's North Carolina Tour," in the *Booker T. Washington Papers*, ed. Louis R. Harlan, Raymond W. Smock, and Geraldine McTighe, 14 vols. (Urbana: University of Illinois Press, 1972–1989), 10:455–61.

2. Along with Shepard, Washington's North Carolina contingency included the Right Reverend Bishop George W. Clinton of the A.M.E. Zion Church of North Carolina, John Merrick and C. C. Spaulding of the North Carolina Mutual and Provident Association, Emmett J. Scott, Washington's private secretary, W. T. McCrorey of Biddle University, E. H. Clement, editor of the Star of Zion and James B. Dudley, president of North Carolina Agricultural and Mechanical College.

3. Leslie Brown, *Upbuilding Black Durham: Gender, Class and Black Community Development in the Jim Crow South* (Chapel Hill: University of North Carolina Press, 2009), 170–71.

4. Ibid.

5. Stephen James Nelson, *Leaders in the Crucible: The Moral Voice of College Presidents* (Westport, CT: Bergin and Garvey Press, 2000), 3.

6. Eric Anderson and Alfred A. Moss, Jr., *Dangerous Donations: Northern Philanthropy and Southern Black Education, 1902–1930* (Columbia: University of Missouri Press, 1999), 16–19. Morris L. Davis, *The Methodist Unification: Christianity and the Politics of Race in the Jim Crow Era* (New York: New York University Press, 2008), 63–65.

7. James E. Shepard to Benjamin Newton Duke, February 8, 1911, B. N. Duke Papers. Stephanie J. Shaw, *What a Woman Ought to Be and Do: Black Women Workers During the Jim Crow Era* (Chicago: University of Chicago Press, 1996), 1–104; Jacqueline Anne Rouse, *Lugenia Burns Hope: Black Southern Reformer* (Athens: University of Georgia Press, 1989), 57–90. James L. Leloudis, *Schooling the New South: Pedagogy, Self, and Society in North Carolina, 1880–1920* (Chapel Hill: University of North Carolina Press, 1996), 177–228.

8. *Pittsburgh Courier*, March 27, 1911.

9. Ibid., September 23, 1911.

10. Brown's *Upbuilding Black Durham*.

11. *Pittsburgh Courier*, November 18, 1911.

12. Ibid.

13. Ibid. Refer to chapter one to gain a fuller understanding of the author's argument of the "civilizing mission" and the use of it by black college presidents during the late nineteenth and early twentieth centuries. It is also important to note that Booker T. Washington actually endorsed James E. Shepard as the president of the NRTIC during its infancy. "Durham, North Carolina, A City of Negro Enterprise," March 30, 1911, in the *Booker T. Washington Papers*, ed. Louis R. Harlan, Raymond W. Smock, and Geraldine McTighe, 14 vols. (Urbana: University of Illinois Press, 1972–1989), 11:61.

14. L. Davis, *A Clashing of the Soul*, 129–83; Benjamin E. Mays, *Born to Rebel: An Autobiography* (Athens: University of Georgia Press, 2003), 89–195. James E. Shepard to Major John C. Hemphill, December 2, 1911, Hemphill Papers.

15. James E. Shepard to J. C. Hemphill, December 2, 1911, Hemphill Papers.

16. Darlene Clarke Hine, William C. Hine, and Stanley Harrold, *The African American Odyssey: Combined Volume* (Upper Saddle River, NJ: Prentice Hall, 2008), 418.

17. J. C. Hemphill to James E. Shepard, December 16, 1912, Hemphill Papers; Beverly W. Jones, "James Edward Shepard, "The Founder: An Educational and Community Leader and Fundraiser," *A History of N. C. Central University: A Town and Gown Analysis* (Durham, NC: North Carolina Humanities Committee, 1985), 13.

18. *Pittsburgh Courier*, March 9, 1912.

19. Ibid.

20. Ibid.; Nicholas Lemann, *The Promise Land: The Great Black Migration and How It Changed America* (New York: Alfred A. Knopf, 1991).

21. Lemann, *Promise Land*.

22. Ibid.

23. David Sehat, "The Civilizing Mission of Booker T. Washington," *Journal of Southern History* (May 2007): 1–30; Booker T. Washington, "The Colored Ministry: Its Defects and Needs," *The Christian Union* (August 14, 1890).

24. Kenneth Goings, "They Dared to Call Their Souls Their Own: The Classics as a Tool of Resistance and Social Uplift" (article publication forthcoming). According to Goings, a number of the "Negro Colleges" trained their students in Greek and Latin as a way to display their intelligence to the larger society. Moreover, African American intellectuals argued that

there was a connection between ancient African societies and those of ancient European empires; therefore, many of the students during this generation desired to learn these histories and languages as if it were their own.

25. Jones, "The Founder: An Educational and Community Leaders and Fundraiser," 18; Reginald K. Ellis, "Nathan B. Young: Florida A & M College's Second President and His Relationships with White Public Officials," in *Go Sound The Trumpet!: Selections in Florida's African American History*, ed. David H. Jackson Jr. and Canter Brown Jr. (Tampa, FL: University of Tampa Press, 2005), 153–72.

26. Jones, "The Founder," 18; Elizabeth Irene Seay, "A History of the North Carolina College for Negroes" (master thesis, Duke University, 1941), 35.

27. James E. Shepard to B. N. Duke, February 26, 1913, B. N. Duke Papers.

28. James E. Shepard to William Preston Few, December 8, 1914; William Few to James E. Shepard, December 14, 1914; James E. Shepard to William Few, December 18, 1914; all in William Preston Few Records and Papers, Duke University Archives, David M. Rubenstein Rare Book & Manuscript Library, Duke University.

29. James E. Shepard to William Preston Few, December 8, 1914; William Few to James E. Shepard, December 14, 1914; James E. Shepard to William Few, December 18, 1914; all in William Preston Few Records and Papers, Duke University Archives, David M. Rubenstein Rare Book & Manuscript Library, Duke University.

30. Elizabeth Seay, "History of North Carolina College for Negroes," 59–60; Jones, "The Founder," 20–23.

31. Jones, "The Founder," 20–23.

32. Ibid.

33. The other black colleges that were state supported during this era were Fayetteville State, which was originally the Howard School for African Americans founded in 1867; Elizabeth City State, the second publicly funded Black College in North Carolina, was created in 1891 to train African American teachers and Winston Salem State College which was the fourth founded in 1892 by the state of North Carolina with North Carolina Agricultural and Mechanical College serving as the third black college created in 1892.

34. Brown, *Upbuilding Black Durham* 122.

Chapter 4. Behind Enemy Lines with No Beachhead: James E. Shepard's Relationship with the NAACP during the Jim Crow Era

Epigraph source: W. E. B. Du Bois, "The Upbuilding of Black Durham: The Success of the Negroes and their Value to a Tolerant and Helpful Southern City," 336–37.

1. *New Journal and Guide*, January 29, 1927.

2. Ibid.; David H. Jackson Jr., *Booker T. Washington and the Struggle Against White Supremacy: The Southern Educational Tours* (New York: Palgrave McMillan, 2008), 168.

3. Jackson, *Booker T. Washington and the Struggle*, 168.

4. Gerald L. Smith, *A Black Educator Southern in the Segregated South: Kentucky's Rufus B. Atwood* (Lexington: University of Kentucky Press, 1994).

5. Jackson, *Booker T. Washington and the Struggle*, 31–52.

6. James E. Shepard to W. E. B. Du Bois, October 27, 1927, Du Bois Papers. *Norfolk Journal*, November 4, 18, 1916; Brown, *Upbuilding Black Durham*, 122.

7. *Pittsburgh Courier*, June 4, 1927.

8. Ibid.; Jacquelyn Rouse, *Lugenia Burns Hope, Black Southern Reformer* (Athens: University of Georgia Press, 1989); Kelly Miller, "The Harvest of Race Prejudice," *The Survey Graphic*, Harlem (March 1925), 682–83.

9. Walter B. Weare, *Black Business in the New South: A Social History of the North Carolina Mutual Life Insurance Company* (Urbana: University of Illinois Press, 1973), 180.

10. *Pittsburgh Courier*, June 4, 1927.

11. James E. Shepard to W. E. B. Du Bois, August 22, 1927, Du Bois Papers.

12. W. E. B. Du Bois to James E. Shepard, August 26, 1927, Du Bois Papers.

13. James E. Shepard to W. E. B. Du Bois, October 10, 1927, Du Bois Papers.

14. W. E. B. Du Bois to James E. Shepard, October, 13, 1927, Du Bois Papers.

15. Ibid.; *New York Amsterdam News*, September 28, 1927.

16. *News Journal and Guide,* December 17, 1927.

17. Ibid.

18. Raymond Gavins, "Fighting for Civil Rights in the Age of Segregation: The NAACP in North Carolina to 1955" (unpublished essay housed in Reginald K. Ellis's historical collection); *The Crisis*, May 14, 1917.

19. Darlene Clark Hine, William C. Hine, and Stanley Harrold, *The African American Odyssey* (Upper Saddle River, NJ: Prentice Hall, 2010), 433.

20. Ibid.

21. Patricia Sullivan, *Lift Every Voice: The NAACP and the Making of the Civil Rights Movement* (New York: New Press, 2009), 101–44.

22. Ibid., 105.

23. Ibid., 105.

24. Ibid., 107.

25. Ibid.

26. Ibid., 107–9.

27. Harvard Sitkoff, *A New Deal For Blacks: The Emergence of Civil Rights as a National Issue: The Great Depression* (Oxford: Oxford University Press, 2009), 18; Angela Hornsby-Gutting, *Black Manhood and Community Building in North Carolina, 1900–1930* (Gainesville: University Press of Florida, 2009), 124.

28. Hornsby-Gutting, *Black Manhood and Community,* 124.

29. *New Journal and Guild*, January 28, 1928; Tavis Smiley, *The Covenant with Black America* (New York: Third Word Press, 2006); *New York Amsterdam News*, December 12, 1928.

30. *Pittsburgh Courier*, May 5, 1928; *The Nation*, June 26, 1926.

31. *Pittsburgh Courier*, May 5, 1928; *The Nation*, June 26, 1926; John Hope Franklin and Evelyn Brooks Higginbotham, *From Slavery to Freedom: A History of African Americans* (New York: McGraw Hill, 2010), 414–15.

32. *Pittsburgh Courier*, May 5, 1928. The prize for the winning entry was *The Negro in Our History*, by Dr. Carter G. Woodson, and a one-year subscription to *The Messenger* magazine.

33. *New Journal and Guide*, March 31, 1928; *Chicago Defender*, April 7, 1928.

34. *New Journal and Guide*, March 31, 1928.

35. Ibid. For more historical insight on the Teapot Dome scandal, please refer to Laton McCartney, *The Teapot Dome Scandal: How Big Oil Bought the Harding White House and Tried to Steal the Country* (New York: Random House, 2009).

36. *New Journal and Guild,* March 31, 1928.

37. Ibid.; Interview with Dr. John Hope Franklin and the author, December 17, 2007, Durham, North Carolina. The notes of this interview are in the possession of the author. Dr. Franklin recalled that every week Dr. Shepard would address the faculty, staff, and student body of NCC and on occasion would not necessarily be prepared. According to Franklin, he always knew when Shepard did not have a written address prepared because he would begin the speech by proclaiming that "this morning I am going to speak from the fullness of my heart." Although Shepard surely had a prepared statement for his audience at Duke University, it is likely that he also spoke from the "fullness of his heart" when it came to addressing the issue of race in America.

38. *Chicago Defender,* September 28, 1928.

39. *New York Amsterdam News*, December 12, 1928; *Philadelphia Tribune*, December 13, 1928.

40. *Pittsburgh Courier*, March 2, 1929.

41. Ibid.

42. *New Journal and Guide,* April 6, 1929.

43. *Pittsburgh Courier*, May 18, 1929.

44. Ibid.

45. *Chicago Defender,* July 27, 1929; *Pittsburgh Courier,* November 9, 1929.

46. Kenneth Robert Janken, *Walter White: Mr. NAACP* (Chapel Hill: University of North Carolina Press, 2003), 157–62.

47. Franklin and Higginbotham, *From Slavery to Freedom,* 436–37.

48. Ibid.

49. Ibid.

50. Janken, *Walter White,* 167.

51. Ibid.

52. Ibid., 167–69.

53. Ibid., 169.

54. Leslie Brown, *Upbuilding Black Durham,* 309–30; Janken, *Walter White,* 184–86; Glenda Elizabeth Gilmore, *Defying Dixie: The Radical Roots of Civil Rights, 1919–1950* (New York: W. W. Norton, 2008), 265–64.

55. Janken, *Walter White,* 199–260.

56. Amilcar Shabazz, *Advancing Democracy: African Americans and the Struggle for Access and Equity in Higher Education in Texas* (Chapel Hill: University of North Carolina Press, 2004), 34–65.

57. Ibid.

58. Ibid.

59. Conrad O. Pearson to Walter White, March 31, 1933, Walter Francis White and Poppy Cannon Papers, Yale Collection of American Literature, Beinecke Rare Book and Manuscript Library, Yale University; Gilbert Ware, "*Hocutt:* Genesis of *Brown,*" *Journal of Negro Education* 52, no. 5 (Summer 1983): 227–33.

60. Weare, *Black Business in the New South,* 209–64); Brown, *Upbuilding Black Durham* (309–30).

61. Shepard to Nathan C. Newbold, February 17, 1933, Department of Public Instruction, Division of Negro Education, General Correspondence of the Director, North Carolina Department of Archives and History, Raleigh, NC; Augustus M. Burns III, "Graduate Edu-

cation for Blacks in North Carolina, 1930–1951," *Journal of Southern History* 46, no. 2 (May 1980): 197.

62. "Graduate Education for Blacks in North Carolina," 197.

Chapter 5. Are You For Me or Against Me? The Political Life of James E. Shepard

Epigraph source: Rob Christensen, *The Paradox of Tar Heel Politics: The Personalities, Elections, and Events that Shaped Modern North Carolina* (Chapel Hill: University of North Carolina Press, 2008), 4.

1. Kenneth Goings, *The NAACP Comes of Age* (Bloomington: Indiana University Press, 1990), 3; Nancy J. Weiss, *Farewell to the Party of Lincoln: Black Politics in the Age of FDR* (Princeton, NJ: Princeton University Press, 1983), 4; John Hope Franklin and Evelyn Brook Higginbotham, *From Slavery to Freedom: A History of African Americans* (Boston: McGraw Hill, 2010), 540.

2. Franklin and Higginbotham, *From Slavery to Freedom*, 540.

3. Ibid.

4. *Afro-American*, April 12, 1930; Vladimir O. Key, *Southern Politics: In State and Nation* (New York: Alfred A. Knopf, 1950), 220.

5. Key, *Southern Politics*, 220.

6. Ibid.

7. Goings, *"The NAACP Coming of Age,"* 22.

8. Ibid., 19–34.

9. Ibid., 23.

10. Ibid., 26–29.

11. Ibid.

12. Ibid.; *Pittsburgh Courier*, June 28, 1930; Sherman, *The Republican Party and Black America*, 241.

13. Goings, *"The NAACP Coming of Age,"* 28; *Pittsburgh Courier*, June 28, 1930; *Baltimore Afro American*, April 12, 1930; James E. Shepard to Lee S. Overman, March 29, 1930, John Johnston Parker Papers, 1906–1987, Southern Historical Collection, University of North Carolina at Chapel Hill. Kenneth Goings, *The NAACP Comes of Age*, argues that the John J. Parker case catapulted Walter White and the NAACP into national prominence as they were able to help defeat Parker's confirmation to the Supreme Court with the support of the American Federation of Labor (AFL); Janken, *Walter White*, (Chapel Hill: University of North Carolina Press, 2003), 140–45.

14. *Pittsburgh Courier*, April 26, 1930.

15. Ibid.

16. Ibid.; Goings, *The NAACP Comes of Age*, 24.

17. Goings, *The NAACP Comes of Age*, 24.

18. Ibid.; Finding Aid, The National Association for the Advancement of Colored People Papers, Group I, Series 211 (hereafter NAACP), University of California, Berkeley. Although Shepard did not win the Spingarn Medal in 1926 (Carter G. Woodson was the winner of the award that year), the fact that he was nominated speaks volumes about the respect that he garnered from the Spingarn Medal committee; L. Davis, *A Clashing of the Soul*, 215.

19. *Baltimore Afro-American*, May 3, 1930.

20. Ibid.

21. Ibid. With the success of disenfranchisement of black males in North Carolina by 1900, a young James E. Shepard issued an angry statement on their behalf. "We recognize the fact there can be no middle ground between freedom and slavery," Shepard argued. Finishing this fiery statement, he asserted, "We cannot see that the best way to make a good man is to unman him."

22. *Baltimore Afro-American*, May 3, 1930.

23. *Chicago Defender,* July 12, 1930; Reginald K. Ellis, "Behind Enemy Lines with no Beach Head: The "Gradual Race Philosophy of James E. Shepard during the Jim Crow Era," unpublished essay housed in the author's historical collection.

24. *Pittsburgh Courier,* June 28, 1930.

25. *Pittsburgh Courier*, August 12, 1933. Harvard Sitkoff, *A New Deal for Blacks: The Emergence of Civil Rights as a National Issue: The Depression Decade* (New York: Oxford University Press, 1928), 74.

26. James E. Shepard to John J. Parker, October 10, 1933, Race Relations Files, Johnson Papers; John J. Parker to James E. Shepard, October 12, 1933, Johnson Papers.

27. James E. Shepard to John J. Parker, October 16, 1933; John J. Parker to James E. Shepard, October 19, 1933; James E. Shepard to John J. Parker, October 23, 1933; all in Johnson Papers.

28. D. O. W. Holmes, "The Negro College Faces the Depression," *Journal of Negro Education* 2, no. 1 (January 1933): 16–25.

29. Ibid.

30. *Chicago Defender*, May 25, 1935; *Pittsburgh Courier*, May 25, 1935.

31. *Pittsburgh Courier,* December 14, 1935.

32. Ibid; Goings, *The NAACP Comes of Age*, 3. *Pittsburgh Courier*, December 14, 1935; Goings, *"NAACP Comes of Age,"* 3; Sitkoff, *A New Deal for Blacks*, 34–44.

33. Janken, *Walter White: Mr. NAACP*, 36–37, 69–70.

34. David A. Lane Jr., "The Report of the National Advisory Committee on Education and the Problem of Negro Education," *Journal of Negro Education*, 1, no.1 (1932), 5–15.

35. Ibid.

36. Ibid.

37. *Cleveland Call and Post*, January 23, 1936; *New Journal and Guide*, January 25, 1936.

38. *Chicago Defender*, February 1, 1936; *Pittsburgh Courier,* February 1, 1936.

39. *Chicago Defender*, May 30, 1936.

40. Ibid.

41. Ibid.

42. Charles A. Jones to A. M. Curtis, July 17, 1936, Republican Party-Colored Division Papers, in the Charles Andrew Jonas Papers #4536, Southern Historical Collection, The Wilson Library, University of North Carolina at Chapel Hill. According to Jones, there were over forty thousand registered African American voters in North Carolina in 1936, and from his estimate roughly 70 percent of them were voting with the Democratic Party.

43. James E. Shepard to Charles A. Jones, October 29, 1936, ibid.

44. *Atlanta Daily World*, March 15, 1937; *Cleveland Call and Post*, March 18, 1937.

45. *Atlanta Daily World,* September 19, 1937; *Chicago Defender*, September 25, 1937; *New Journal and Guide*, October 2, 1937.

46. *Baltimore Afro-American*, December 11, 1937.

47. Ibid.

48. *Atlanta Daily World*, December 9, 1937.

49. *Afro-American World,* December 11, 1937.

Chapter 6. "Don't Crash the Gate but Stand on Your Own Feet!": Shepard and his Legacy

1. Glenda Elizabeth Gilmore, *Defying Dixie: The Radical Roots of Civil Rights: 1919–1950* (New York: W. W. Norton, 2008), 263–64.

2. Ibid., 273. Although Shepard shielded Graham in 1933 by not releasing Thomas Hocutt's transcript and again in 1939 by not serving as an open advocate for integrated higher education, UNC's president received his share of criticism, although the brunt of the blame was directed toward Shepard. From this researcher's perspective, these individuals needed each other to survive the pre–civil rights movements not only for the protection of NCC but for the survival of their careers as administrators in general. Once the early attempts at integration subsided, Graham was "forcible coxed" by Governor Scott Kerr to step outside of his comfort zone and enter politics by running for the United States Senate. Away from the shield of the ivory tower, Graham's liberal policies were thoroughly examined. Many white North Carolinians, nevertheless, felt that his views of race relations were too liberal and were out of step with his constituency. Graham eventually saw the backlash for his liberal ways during his campaign for the United States Senate in 1950, as his opponents labeled him a socialist and black sympathizer, which in many ways damaged Graham's legacy for generations.

3. Gilmore, *Defying Dixie*, 264–65; Adam Fairclough, *A Class of Their Own: Black Teachers in the Segregated South* (Cambridge, MA: Harvard University Press, 2007), 363; Amilcar Shabazz, *Advancing Democracy: African Americans and the Struggle for Access and Equality in Higher Education in Texas* (Chapel Hill: University of North Carolina Press, 2004).

4. Shabazz, *Advancing Democracy*, 265–66; James L. Leloudis, *Schooling the New South: Pedagogy, Self and Society in North Carolina, 1880–1920* (Chapel Hill: University of North Carolina Press, 1996), 177–228.

5. Gilmore, *Defying Dixie*, 266.

6. Ibid.

7. Ibid.; 284; *New Journal and Guide*, July 9, 1938.

8. Gilmore, *Defying Dixie*, 284; Augustus M. Bush III, "Graduate Education for Blacks in North Carolina, 1930–1951," *Journal of Southern History* 46, no. 2 (May 1980): 205–7.

9. James E. Shepard to F. P. Keppel, November 6, 1940, Series 2.1, Request Received for Information and Assistance File, Johnson Papers.

10. *Chicago Defender,* February 18, 1939.

11. Gilmore, *Defying Dixie*, 234; Guy B. Johnson to James E. Shepard, March 9, 1943, Series 2.1, North Carolina College for Negroes file, Johnson Papers.

12. Guy B. Johnson, "Summary of Reaction of Individual States as Research by Check List Since the *Gaines* and *Alston* decision," Johnson Papers.

13. Ibid.

14. Ibid. In an article titled "The Negro College," in *The Crisis*, August 1933, W. E. B. Du

Bois argued that if African Americans did not receive the same quality of education that their white peers received not only would the black community fail but the South as a whole would continue to lag behind the nation economically.

15. Marc Gallicchio, *The African American Encounter with Japan and China: Black Internationalism in Asia, 1895–1945* (Chapel Hill: University of North Carolina Press, 2000), 1. John Hope Franklin and Evelyn Brooks Higginbotham, *From Slavery to Freedom: A History of African Americans*, 9th edition (New York: McGraw Hill, 2010), 451.

16. *Atlanta Daily World*, October 18, 1943.

17. Ibid.

18. Franklin and Higginbotham, *From Slavery to Freedom*, 451, 470–71.

19. *Chicago Defender*, February 19, 1944.

20. *Chicago Defender*, February 26, 1944.

21. *Atlanta Daily World*, March 15, 1944.

22. Ibid.

23. Ibid.

24. *Atlanta Daily World*, May 2, 1944.

25. Ibid.

26. Ibid.

27. Nathan C. Newbold to Frank Porter Graham, May 22, 1944, Series 1819, 1944, Negroes and Race Relations File, Graham Papers. Nathan C. Newbold to Frank Porter Graham, June 12, 1944, Graham Papers.

28. Nathan C. Newbold to Frank Porter Graham, June 12, 1944, Graham Papers.

29. James E. Shepard to Frank Porter Graham, July 22, 1944, Graham Papers.

30. Ibid.

31. Frank Porter Graham to James E. Shepard, August 1, 1944, Graham Papers.

32. Ibid.

33. *The Crisis*, October 1944.

34. Ibid.

35. Ibid.

36. Ibid.

37. Ibid.

38. Ibid.

39. Ibid.

40. James E. Shepard to Frank Graham, September 1, 1944, Graham Papers.

41. Ibid. After the first Stock-Taking conference, James Shepard gained the leadership role of this racial think tank while C. C. Spaulding served as the treasure of this organization.

42. James E. Shepard to N. C. Newbold, September 20, 1944, Graham Papers.

43. Frank Graham to James E. Shepard, September 25, 1944, Graham Papers.

44. C. C. Spaulding to Frank Graham, October 14, 1944, Graham Papers; *The Crisis*, October 1944.

45. *New York Amsterdam News*, March 25, 1945.

46. *Chicago Defender*, February 23, 1946.

47. Ibid.

48. Ibid.

49. *New York Amsterdam News*, June 8, 1946.

50. *New York Amsterdam News,* February 12 and 15, 1947; *Chicago Defender,* February 22, 1947.

51. Memorial Service Program of Mrs. Hattie E. Shepard, Friday, April 18, 1947, James E. Shepard Papers, 1905–1990, University Archives, Records and History Center in the James E. Shepard Memorial Library, North Carolina Central University.

52. *Atlanta Daily World,* May 2, 1947.

53. "To Secure These Rights: The Report of the President's Committee on Civil Rights," Housed in the Harry S. Truman Presidential Library; Franklin and Moss, *From Slavery to Freedom,* 506.

Epilogue: A Legacy Continued

Epigraph note: Dr. James E. Shepard would often lead his school in this chant at the beginning of each academic year. Not only did this chant serve as motivation, it also provided the president's explanation as to why the Eagle was chosen as the school's mascot.

1. *Pittsburgh Courier,* October 18, 1947.

2. Ibid.

3. Ibid., November 1, 1947.

4. Ibid.

5. *Atlanta Daily World,* January 22, 1948; *The Pittsburgh Courier,* January 31, 1948.

6. *Pittsburgh Courier,* January 31, 1948.

7. *Atlanta Daily World,* February 1, 1948.

8. *Durham Sun,* March 1, 1949.

9. Ibid.

10. Ibid.

11. Ibid.

12. Ibid.

13. Ibid.

14. Ibid.

15. Ibid.

Bibliography

Primary Sources

Allen, Arch T. Papers. North Carolina Superintendent of Public Instruction (1902–1952). State of North Carolina Archives, Raleigh.

Atlanta Daily World

Aycock, Charles Brantley Aycock. Papers. State of North Carolina Archives, Raleigh.

Bickett, Thomas Walter. Papers. State of North Carolina Archives, Raleigh.

Brooks, Eugene C. Papers. North Carolina Superintendent of Public Instruction (1902–1952). State of North Carolina Archives, Raleigh.

Broughton, J. Melville. Papers. State of North Carolina Archives, Raleigh.

Charlotte Gazette (North Carolina).

Cherry, R. Gregg. Papers. State of North Carolina Archives, Raleigh.

Chicago Defender

Craig, Locke. Papers. State of North Carolina Archives, Raleigh.

Dawson, Robert Edward. Papers. Duke University Archives, Durham, NC.

Division of Negro Education Papers, Raleigh, NC.

Du Bois, W. E. B. Papers. Ned R. McWherter Library, University of Memphis, TN.

Duke, Benjamin Newton. Papers. David M. Rubenstein Rare Book & Manuscript Library, Duke University, Durham, NC.

Duke, Washington. Papers. Duke University Archives, Durham, NC.

Durham Carolina Times, NC.

Durham Country Republican, NC.

Durham Daily Sun, NC.

Durham Morning Herald, NC.

Durham Negro Observer, NC.

Durham Tobacco Plant, NC

Ehringhaus, John C. B. Papers. State of North Carolina Archives, Raleigh.

Erwin, Clyde A. Papers. North Carolina Superintendent of Public Instruction (1902–1952). State of North Carolina Archives, Raleigh.

Few, William Preston. Records and Papers. Duke University Archives, David M. Rubenstein Rare Book & Manuscript Library, Duke University, Durham, NC.

Gardner, Oliver Max. Papers. State of North Carolina Archives, Raleigh.

Glenn, Robert Broadnex. Papers. State of North Carolina Archives, Raleigh.

Graham, Frank Porter. Papers. #1819, Southern Historical Collection, The Wilson Library, University of North Carolina at Chapel Hill.

Greensboro Daily News (NC).

Gregory, Edwin Clarke Gregory. Papers. Duke University Archives, Durham, NC.

Hancock, Gordon Blaine. Papers. Duke University Archives, Durham, NC.

Hemphill Family Papers. David M. Rubenstein Rare Book & Manuscript Library, Duke University, Durham, NC.

Hillsborough Recorder (NC).

Hinsdale Family Papers. Duke University Archives, Durham, NC.

Hoey, Clyde R. Papers. State of North Carolina Archives, Raleigh.

Johnson, Guy Benton. Papers. #3826, Southern Historical Collection, The Wilson Library, University of North Carolina at Chapel Hill.

Jonas, Charles Andrew. Papers. #4536, Southern Historical Collection, The Wilson Library, University of North Carolina at Chapel Hill.

Joyner, James Y. Papers. North Carolina Superintendent of Public Instruction (1902–1952). State of North Carolina Archives, Raleigh.

Kennedy, William Jesse. Papers. University of North Carolina, Southern Historical Collection, Chapel Hill.

Kilgo John C. Records and Papers. Duke University Archives, David M. Rubenstein Rare Book & Manuscript Library, Duke University, Durham. NC.

Kitchin, William Walton. Papers. State of North Carolina Archives, Raleigh.

Leuchtenburg, William Edward. Papers. University of North Carolina Southern Historical Collection, Chapel Hill.

McLean, Angus Wilton. Papers. State of North Carolina Archives, Raleigh.

Morrison, Cameron. Papers. State of North Carolina Archives, Raleigh.

Newbold, Nathan C. Papers. Department of Public Instruction, Division of Negro Education, General Correspondence of the Director, North Carolina Department of Archives and History, Raleigh.

Overman, Lee S. Papers. #570, Southern Historical Collection, The Wilson Library, University of North Carolina at Chapel Hill.

Parker, John Johnston. Papers, 1906–1987. Southern Historical Collection, The Wilson Library, University of North Carolina at Chapel Hill.

Pittsburgh Courier

Raleigh News Observer

Shepard, James E.. Papers, 1905–1990. University Archives, Records and History Center in the James E. Shepard Memorial Library, North Carolina Central University, Durham.

Sprunt, Alexander, and Son. Records. David M. Rubenstein Rare Book and Manuscript Library, Duke University, Durham. NC.

Thomas, James Augustus. Papers. Duke University Archives, Durham, NC.

Tompkins, Daniel Augustus. Papers, University of North Carolina, Southern Historical Collection, Chapter Hill.

White, Walter Francis, and Poppy Cannon. Papers. Yale Collection of American Literature, Beinecke Rare Book and Manuscript Library, Yale University, New Haven, CT.

Secondary Sources

Anderson, Eric, and Alfred A. Moss Jr. *Dangerous Donations: Northern Philanthropy and Southern Black Education, 1902–1930.* Columbia: University of Missouri Press, 1999.

Anderson, James D. *The Education of Blacks in the South, 1860–1935*. Chapel Hill: University of North Carolina Press, 1988.

———. "Northern Foundations and the Shaping of Southern Black Rural Education, 1902–1935." *History of Education Quarterly* 18 (1978): 371–96.

Bagby, George F. "Hollis F. Price: Apprenticeship at Tuskegee Institute, 1933–1940." *Alabama Review* 60 (2007): 29–52.

Brown, Leslie. *Upbuilding Black Durham: Gender, Class and Black Community Development in the Jim Crow South*. Chapel Hill: University of North Carolina Press, 2009.

Burns III, Augustus M. "Graduate Education for Blacks in North Carolina, 1930–1951." *Journal of Southern History* 46, no. 2 (May 1980): 195–218.

Butchart, Ronald E. "'Outthinking and Outflanking the Owners of the World': A Historiography of the African American Struggle for Education." *History of Education Quarterly* 28, no. 3 (Autumn 1988): 333–36.

Butler, Anne S. "Black Fraternal and Benevolent Societies in Nineteenth-Century America." in *African American Fraternities and Sororities: The Legacy and the Vision*, edited by Tamara L. Brown, Gregory S. Parks, and Clarenda M. Phillips. Lexington: University of Kentucky Press, 2005.

Cannon, Robert. "The Organization and Growth of Black Political Participation in Durham, North Carolina, 1933–1958." PhD diss., University of North Carolina at Chapel Hill, 1975.

Cecelski, David. *Democracy Betrayed: The Wilmington Race Riot of 1898 and its Legacy* Chapel Hill: University of North Carolina Press, 1998.

Chafe, William H. *Civilities and Civil Rights: Greensboro, North Carolina, and the Black Struggle for Freedom*. Oxford: Oxford University Press, 1980.

Christensen, Rob. *The Paradox of Tar Heel Politics: The Personalities, Elections, and Events that Shaped Modern North Carolina*. Chapel Hill: University of North Carolina Press, 2008.

Chujo, Ken. "The Black Struggle for Education in North Carolina, 1877–1900." PhD diss., Duke University, 1988.

Dagbovie, Pero Gaglo. "Exploring a Century Of Historical Scholarship on Booker T. Washington." *Journal of African American History* 92 (2007): 239–64.

Dailey, Jane. "Deference and Violence in the Postbellum Urban South: Manners and Massacres in Danville, Virginia." *Journal of Southern History* 63 (August 1997): 53–90.

Davis, Leroy. *A Clashing of the Soul: John Hope and the Dilemma of African American Leadership and Black Higher Education in the Early Twentieth Century*. Athens: University of Georgia Press, 1998.

Davis, Morris L. *The Methodist Unification: Christianity and the Politics of Race in the Jim Crow Era*. New York: New York University Press, 2008.

Dixon, Thomas. *The Leopard's Spots: A Romance of the White Man's Burden*. New York: Doubleday, 1902.

Du Bois, W. E. B. *The Education of Black People: Ten Critiques, 1906–1960*. Edited by Herbert Aptheker. Amherst: University of Massachusetts Press, 1973.

———. "The Negro College," *The Crisis* (August 1933).

———. *The Souls of Black Folk*. 1903; New York: Random House Press, 1996.

———. "The Upbuilding of Black Durham: The Success of the Negroes and their Value to a Tolerant and Helpful Southern City," *World's Work* 23 (January 1912): 336–37.

Durden, Robert F. *The Dukes of Durham, 1865–1929*. Durham, NC: Duke University Press, 1975.

Earp, Carolyn Bond. "North Carolina Governors and Public Education, 1933–1961." Master's thesis: Duke University, 1979.

Edgcomb, Gabrielle Simon. *From Swastika to Jim Crow: Refugee Scholars at Black Colleges*. Malabar, FL: Krieger Publishing Company, 1993.

Ellis, Reginald K. "Florida State Normal and Industrial School for Coloreds: Thomas DeSalle Tucker and His Radical Approach to Black Higher Education." Seminar Paper, University of Memphis, TN, 2006.

———. "Nathan B. Young: Florida A&M College's Second President and His Relationships with White Public Officials." In *Go Sound the Trumpet!: Selections in Florida's African American History*, edited by Canter Brown Jr. and David H. Jackson Jr. Tampa, FL: University of Tampa Press, 2005.

Enck, Henry S. "Black Self-Help in the Progressive Era: The 'Northern Campaigns' of Smaller Southern Black Industrial Schools, 1900–1915." *Journal of Negro History* 61 (1976): 73–87.

Fairclough, Adam. "Being in the Field of Education and Also Being a Negro . . . Seems . . . Tragic: Black Teachers in the Jim Crow South." *Journal of American History* 87 (2001): 5–25.

———. *A Class of Their Own: Black Teachers in the Segregated South*. Cambridge, MA: Harvard University Press, 2007.

Foner, Eric. *Reconstruction: America's Unfinished Revolution*. New York: Harper and Row, 1988.

———. *A Short History of Reconstruction: 1863–1877*. New York: Harper and Row, 1990.

Franklin, John Hope. *Mirror to America: The Autobiography of John Hope Franklin*. New York: Farrar, Straus and Giroux Press, 2006.

Franklin, John Hope, and Evelyn Brooks Higginbotham. *From Slavery to Freedom: A History of African Americans* (New York: McGraw Hill Press, 2010).

Franklin, John Hope, and August Meier, eds. *Black Leaders of the Twentieth Century*. Urbana: University of Illinois Press, 1982.

Gaines, Kevin. *Uplifting the Race: Black Leadership, Politics, and Culture in the Twentieth Century*. Chapel Hill: University of North Carolina Press, 1996.

Gallicchio, Marc. *The African American Encounter with Japan and China: Black Internationalism in Asia, 1895–1945*. Chapel Hill: University of North Carolina Press, 2000.

Gardner, Booker T. "The Educational Contributions of Booker T. Washington." *Journal of Negro Education* 44 (1975): 502–18.

Gatewood, Willard B. *Aristocrats of Color: The Black Elite, 1880–1920*. Bloomington: Indiana University Press, 1990.

Gavins, Raymond. "Fighting for Civil Rights in the Age of Segregation: The NAACP in North Carolina to 1955." Unpublished essay housed in Reginald K. Ellis' historical collection.

Gilmore, Glenda Elizabeth. *Defying Dixie: The Radical Roots of Civil Rights, 1919–1950*. New York: W. W. Norton, 2008.

———. *Gender and Jim Crow: Women and the Politics of White Supremacy in North Carolina, 1896–1920*. Chapel Hill: University of North Carolina Press, 1996.

Goings, Kenneth. *The NAACP Comes of Age*. Bloomington: Indiana University Press, 1990.

———. "They Dared to Call Their Souls Their Own: The Classics as a Tool of Resistance and Social Uplift." Forthcoming.

Gray White, Deborah. *Aren't I a Woman: Female Slaves in the Plantation South.* New York: W. W. Norton, 1985.

———. *Too Heavy a Load: Black Women in Defense of Themselves: 1894–1994.* London: W. W. Norton, 1999.

Greene, Christina. *Our Separate Ways: Women and the Black Freedom Movement in Durham, North Carolina.* Chapel Hill: University of North Carolina Press, 2005.

Hahn, Steven. *A Nation Under Our Feet: Black Political Struggle in The Rural South From Slavery to the Great Migration.* Cambridge, MA: Harvard University Press, 2003.

Harlan, Lewis R. *Booker T. Washington: The Wizard of Tuskegee.* New York: University of Oxford Press, 1983.

———. "Booker T. Washington and the White Man's Burden." *American Historical Review* 71, no. 2 (January 1966): 441–67.

Higginbotham, Evelyn Brooks. *Righteous Discontent: The Women's Movement in the Black Baptist Church, 1880–1920.* Cambridge, MA: Harvard University Press, 1993.

Hixson Jr., William B. "Moorfield Storey and the Defense of the Dyer Anti-Lynching Bill." *New England Quarterly* 42, no. 1 (March 1969): 65–81.

Holland, Antonio F. *Nathan B. Young and the Struggle Over Black Higher Education.* Columbia: University of Missouri Press. 2006.

Holmes, D. O. W. "The Negro College Faces the Depression." *Journal of Negro Education* 2, no. 1 (January 1933): 16–25.

Hornsby-Gutting, Angela. *Black Manhood and Community Building in North Carolina, 1900–1930.* Gainesville: University Press of Florida, 2009.

Jackson Jr., David H. "Booker T. Washington's Tour of the Sunshine State, March 1912." *Florida Historical Quarterly* 81 (Winter 2003): 254–78.

———. *Booker T. Washington and the Struggle against White Supremacy: The Southern Educational Tours.* New York: Palgrave McMillan, 2008.

———. *A Chief Lieutenant of the Tuskegee Machine: Charles Banks of Mississippi.* Gainesville: University Press of Florida, 2002.

Janken, Kenneth Robert. *Walter White: Mr. NAACP.* Chapel Hill: University of North Carolina Press, 2003.

Johnson, James Weldon. *The Autobiography of an Ex-Coloured Man.* New York: Alfred A Knopf, 1927.

Jones, Beverly W. "James Edward Shepard, The Founder: An Educational and Community Leaders and Fundraiser." In *A History of N. C. Central University: A Town and Gown Analysis:* by Beverly W. Jones Durham: North Carolina Humanities Committee, 1985.

Kelley, Blair L. M. *Right to Ride: Streetcar Boycotts and African American Citizenship in the Era of Plessy v. Ferguson.* Chapel Hill: University of North Carolina Press, 2010.

Kennedy Jr, William J. *The North Carolina Mutual Story: A Symbol of Progress, 1890–1970* Durham: North Carolina Mutual Life Insurance Company, 1970.

Key, Vladimir O. *Southern Politics: In State and Nation.* New York: Alfred A. Knopf Press, 1950.

Lane Jr., David A. "The Report of the National Advisory Committee on Education and the Problem of Negro Education." *Journal of Negro Education* 1 (1932): 5–15.

Leloudis, James L. *Schooling the New South: Pedagogy, Self, and Society in North Carolina, 1880–1920*. Chapel Hill: University of North Carolina Press, 1996.

Lemann, Nicholas. *The Promise Land: The Great Black Migration and How It Changed America*. New York: Alfred A. Knopf, 1991.

Lewis, David Levering. *W. E. B. Du Bois: Biography of a Race*. New York: Henry Holt Company, 1993.

Lewis, William H. "An Account of Washington's North Carolina Tour." In *Booker T. Washington Papers*, edited by Louis R. Harlan, Raymond W. Smock, and Geraldine McTighe, 14 vols. (Urbana: University of Illinois Press, 1972–1989: 10: 455–61.

Long, Hollis Moody. *Public Secondary Education for Negroes in North Carolina*. New York: Bureau of Publications, Teachers College, Columbia University, 1932.

Lutz, Tom, and Susanna Ashton, eds. *These "Colored" United States: African American Essays from the 1920s*. New Brunswick, NJ: Rutgers University Press, 1996.

Marlowe, Gertrude Woodruff. *A Right Worthy Grand Mission: Maggie Lena Walker and the Quest for Black Economic Empowerment*. Washington DC: Howard University Press, 2003.

Mays, Benjamin E. *Born to Rebel: An Autobiography*. Athens: University of Georgia Press, 2003.

McCartney, Laton. *The Teapot Dome Scandal: How Big Oil Bought the Harding White House and Tried to Steal the Country*. New York: Random House Trade Paperbacks, 2009.

Miller, Kelly. "The Harvest of Race Prejudice." *The Survey Graphic* (Harlem, NY), March 1925.

Moses, M. Iya-Ilu. "Universal Education for African-Americans in North Carolina: A Historical Survey of the Beginning Years through 1927." PhD diss., North Carolina State University, 1989.

Nelson, Stephen James. *Leaders in the Crucible: The Moral Voice of College Presidents*. Westport, CT: Bergin and Garvey Press, 2000.

Pleasants, Julian M., and August M. Burns. *Frank Porter Graham and the 1950 Senate Race in North Carolina*. Chapel Hill: University of North Carolina Press. 1990.

Price, David Hyde. "A History of the State Department of Public Instruction in North Carolina, 1852–1956." PhD diss., University of North Carolina, 1959.

Rabinowitz, Howard N. "A Comparative Perspective on Race Relations in Southern and Northern Cities 1860–1900, with Special Emphasis on Raleigh." In *Black Americans in North Carolina and the South*, edited by Jeffrey Crow and Flora J. Hatley. 137–59. Chapel Hill: University of North Carolina Press, 1984.

Ransby, Barbara. *Ella Baker and the Black Freedom Movement: A Radical Democratic Vision*. Chapel Hill: University of North Carolina Press. 2003.

Reid, George W. "James E. Shepard and the Public Record of the Founding of North Carolina College at Durham: 1909–1948," *Negro History Bulletin* 41, no. 6 (1978): 900–902.

Richardson, Joe M. *Christian Reconstruction: The American Missionary Association and Southern Blacks, 1861–1890*. Athens: University of Georgia Press, 1996.

Rouse, Jacqueline Anne. *Lugenia Burns Hope: Black Southern Reformer*. Athens: University of Georgia Press, 1989.

Sanders, Crystal R. *A Chance for Change: Head Start and Mississippi's Black Freedom Struggle*. Chapel Hill: University of North Carolina Press, 2016.

Savitt, Todd L. "The Education of Physicians at Shaw University, 1882–1918: Problems of Quality and Quantity." In *Black Americans in North Carolina and the South,* edited by Jeffrey Crow and Flora J. Hatley, 160–88. Chapel Hill: University of North Carolina Press, 1984.

Seay, Elizabeth Irene. "A History of the North Carolina College for Negroes." Master's thesis, Duke University, 1941.

Sehat, David. "The Civilizing Mission of Booker T. Washington." *Journal of Southern History* 73, no. 2 (May 2007): 1–30.

Shabazz, Amilcar. *Advancing Democracy: African Americans and the Struggle for Access and Equity in Higher Education in Texas.* Chapel Hill: University of North Carolina Press, 2004.

Shaw, Stephanie J. *What a Woman Ought to Be and to Do: Black Professional Women Workers during the Jim Crow Era.* Chicago: University of Chicago Press, 1996.

Sitkoff, Harvard. *A New Deal For Blacks: The Emergence of Civil Rights as a National Issue: The Great Depression.* Oxford: Oxford University Press, 2009.

Slinkard, Tomas R. *Public Education in North Carolina during the Depression, 1929–1933.* Master's thesis, University of North Carolina at Chapel Hill, 1948.

Smiley, Tavis. *The Covenant with Black America.* New York: Third Word Press, 2006.

Smith, Gerald L. *A Black Educator in the Segregated South: Kentucky's Rufus B. Atwood.* Lexington: University of Kentucky Press, 1994.

Sullivan, Patricia. *Lift Every Voice: The NAACP and the Making of the Civil Rights Movement.* New York: The New Press, 2009.

Tate, Cassandra. *Cigarette Wars: The Triumph of "The Little White Slaver."* Oxford: Oxford University Press, 1999.

Taylor, Ula Yvette. *The Veiled Garvey: The Life and Times of Amy Jacques Garvey.* Chapel Hill: University of North Carolina Press. 2002.

Thuesen, Sarah Caroline. *Greater Thank Equal: African American Struggles for Schools and Citizenship in North Carolina, 1919–1965.* Chapel Hill: University of North Carolina Press, 2013.

Ware, Gilbert. "*Hocutt:* Genesis of *Brown.*" *Journal of Negro Education* 52, no. 5 (Summer 1983): 227–33.

Washington, Booker T. "The Colored Ministry: Its Defects and Needs." *The Christian Union,* August 14, 1890.

———. *Up From Slavery: An Autobiography.* 1901; New York: Random House, 1999.

Weare, Walter B. *Black Business in the New South: A Social History of the North Carolina Mutual Life Insurance Company.* Urbana: University of Chicago Press, 1973.

Weaver, Garrett. The Development of the Black Community, 1880–1915. PhD diss, University of North Carolina Press at Chapel Hill, 1987.

Weiss, Nancy J. *Farewell to the Party of Lincoln: Black Politics in the Age of FDR.* Princeton, NJ: Princeton University Press, 1983.

Westin, Richard Barry. "The State and Segregated Schools: Negro Public Education in North Carolina, 1863–1923." PhD diss., Duke University, 1966.

Whitted, J. A. *Biographical Sketch of the Life and Work of the Late Rev. Augustus Shepard, D.D., Durham, North Carolina.* Raleigh, NC: Edwards and Broughton Printing Company, 1912.

Woodward, C. Vann. *The Strange Career of Jim Crow.* Oxford: Oxford University Press, 1974.

Zaki, Hoda M. *Civil Rights and Politics at Hampton Institute: The Legacy of Alonzo G. Moron.* Urbana: University of Illinois Press, 2007.

Index

REGINALD K. ELLIS is associate professor of history and African American studies at Florida A&M University. His research specialty is the history of black colleges and universities in general and black college presidents during the Jim Crow era in particular.

CPSIA information can be obtained
at www.ICGtesting.com
Printed in the USA
LVOW12*0831241017

552919LV00002BA/7/P

9 780813 056609